The American Nightmare

The American Nightmare

Don DeLillo's Falling Man
and
Cormac McCarthy's The Road

ÖZDEN SÖZALAN

authorHOUSE®

AuthorHouse™
1663 Liberty Drive
Bloomington, IN 47403
www.authorhouse.com
Phone: 1-800-839-8640

First published by AuthorHouse   09/14/2011

ISBN: 978-1-4567-9814-7 (sc)
ISBN: 978-1-4567-9815-4 (ebk)

Printed in the United States of America

This one is for Edibe

CONTENTS

....

ACKNOWLEDGEMENTS

· ·

I would like to acknowledge my enormous debt to all my colleagues at the Department of American Culture and Literature at Istanbul University. My appreciation to Professor Ayşe Erbora for the support she has given me throughout my academic career. I am short for words to express my gratitude to Associate Professor Hasine Şen and Dr. Cenk Yay, for their invaluable assistance and constant encouragement during the writing of this book. Very big thanks to you, Hasine, for taking the time to read every single draft of my work and provide me with some engaging feedback. And Cenk, I have been lucky to have your devoted and generous editorial assistance all along the way. What greater reward for a teacher to see her favorite student of years ago as a competent academician with skills far exceeding those of his teacher.

My appreciation to all of my family whom I have missed very much during the writing of this book, especially my mother, Sevim, and my father, Hulusi. Their wisdom, tolerance and sense of justice have profoundly shaped my views of life and the world.

I have always been fortunate in friendships that stand the test of time. Affan, I remain grateful that I have had the good fortune to have you as a constant source of love and support in my life. Edibe, my beautiful, good-hearted friend, I thank you with all my heart for your constant encouragement during the writing of this book, at a time when you yourself needed encouragement in your struggle with a life-threatening illness. Billur, you have always been so supporting and giving that I often feel guilty for taking your presence in my life for granted, for not being able to return your kindness and generosity. Additional thanks to you for providing me with some of the source materials for this book, and patiently going over my unintelligible bibliographical references.

Last but not the least, I owe special thanks to two other friends; to Ibrahim, who encouraged me to take on literature as my vocation years ago, and who has since continued to support me in every possible way, and to Saime, for the sister I have found in her, and for her unwavering faith in me. Without you two, neither this book nor my previous works would have been possible. Özden Sözalan. Istanbul, 2011.

INTRODUCTION

. . . .

*If everything were transparent, then no ideology would be
possible, and no domination either.*
—Jameson, *The Political Unconscious*

Probably, there is no other concept more exploited, explored, questioned,
demystified or deconstructed by the literary imagination, and by the tools
of literary criticism, than the infamous "American Dream" whose failure
has been pointed at every drastic turn of American history marked as a
moment of crisis—the Civil War, the Great Depression, and the Vietnam
War, to name a few. The post-9/11 fiction contributed to the literary
preoccupation with the "Dream" from within its own narrative paradigm
stipulating the terms of its confrontation with an unprecedented event that
was perceived to have brought "America under attack". What seems to be
new in the articulations of a shattered dream in post-9/11 narratives is the
transformation of the dream into a nightmare registered in the semantic
and ideological complexities of these texts. This, of course, has to do with
the specificity of the event; the destruction of the twin towers which were,
in the words of Habermas, "a powerful embodiment of economic strength
and *projection toward the future,*" annulled any projection toward the
future based on the strength of the world's leading economy.[1]

The collapse of the Twin Towers on September 11, 2001 was
immediately imprinted on public consciousness as a moment of radical
historical change, variously defined as "America's entry into world
history," or "the end of the American holiday from history," implicating
the American subject in a period of transition marked by violence and
pain. Literary response to the event has focused primarily on its traumatic

impact on the American subject, evidenced in a considerably huge body of texts classified under the heading "post-9/11 fiction" indulging in loss of innocence narratives. Consequently, the child or the adult metaphorically reduced to a child-like state of incomprehension emerges as the protagonist in many novels written in response to the event. Jonathan Safran Foer's *Extremely Loud and Incredibly Close* provides the most distinct example of such a trend with its boy-hero who, having lost his father in the attacks on the towers, tries to restore life to its pre-9/11 state of blissful innocence confined to the sphere of the private/domestic. Innocence, however, entails ignorance as well, and in the last analysis the fictional engagement with psychological aftereffects in such narratives seems to be not only an abortive attempt at a proper working through of trauma, but to have been marked with a persistent refusal to involve with the political historical implications of the event. Novels such as Foer's *Extremely Loud and Incredibly Close*, or Claire Messud's *The Emperor's Children*, significant though in their account of personal experience of loss and ensuing pain against a backdrop of public inscriptions of 9/11 as national tragedy and collectivized trauma, nevertheless end up reinstating the hegemonic discourse instrumentalizing trauma as they lack the clarity of vision that would assess the event's significance in world history.

The so-called entry into world history—was the U.S. ever outside world history?—becomes, therefore, a fall into the end of history in literature produced after September 11, 2001, grieving over a loss which it cannot adequately name or contextualize. The image of the falling towers compounded by the images of people falling from the towers to their death has provided a visual metaphor for the numerous falls experienced in post-9/11 narratives in which the descent from innocence to experience and to knowledge is treated in terms of a continuous fall. The suspension of movement and action on the part of the characters in these narratives is revealing of the limits of a specific ideological consciousness the texts embody. If the fall comes to an end at all its destination is a none-place outside history, following the trajectory of the literal fall that has ended in the emblematic void conveniently named Ground Zero. Hence the end-of-history and the end-of-the-world narratives marked by the limits of the ideological frame in which they are produced and beyond which they cannot go. And it is to that ideological frame informing the text's manifest political horizons that I turn my gaze in the following study.

I have chosen to limit my discussion to the two novels that I view as initiating and concluding the literary descent of the American subject into a world perceived to be no more: Don DeLillo's *Falling Man* inscribes the beginning of the downward journey quite literally in the moment of the fall which is 9/11, while Cormac McCarthy's *The Road*, although appearing a year earlier, carries the theme to the ultimate point of entropy where not only the subject but the whole world is annihilated. There is no reference to 9/11 in McCarthy's dystopian tale of pilgrims in an utterly devastated world, yet its wandering characters follow from where DeLillo leaves his hero practically homeless in a world which has lost its referential value. The popular inscriptions of the suicide attacks on the World Trade Center as a strike at the heart of the nation permeate both texts in which the absent presence of home signifies the disappearance of homeland as a secure place in American cultural imagination. The question one character asks in *Falling Man*, "What comes after America?" (192), is the dreaded question both of these novels attempt to answer, albeit in their similarly pessimistic yet differently articulated political visions. In *Falling Man* the answer comes from a radical activist turned international art dealer: "There is an empty space where America used to be" (193). The titular road in McCarthy's novel snakes through a nightmarish landscape where not only America, but suggestedly the world also used to be. When America is no more, the world itself ceases to exist. This is truly an American nightmare.

A distinctive characteristic of the novels I have chosen for discussion is their efficiency of language with which they paradoxically comment on the failure of language at a moment of crisis. DeLillo's narration enacts the experience of trauma that resists articulation and is replete with fissures and discontinuities that give away what the ideological system of the text represses. McCarthy's poetic narrative which blends a number of expressive modes points more forcefully than DeLillo's to the collapse of the symbolic order, and its language is rich with nightmarish images that irrupt into the surface of the text apropos of the intrusion of the Real into the Symbolic.

I see the unique historical specificity of these novels not in terms of the old historicist reading of literary texts as reflecting a reality to which they are extrinsically related; my concern is rather with the ways in which they interact, in their linguistic and stylistic capacities, with the other texts of "9/11" and its aftermath; the (verbal and visual) textual inscriptions of the event that have instrumentalized trauma, the Patriot Act, the rhetoric of "Us and Them", the "Axis of Evil" and the "War on Terror" that have been used to justify the invasion of Afghanistan and Iraq. DeLillo's narrativization of trauma negates the alternative involving the cultivation of a healthy political public space, as Arendt would have it, as a response to terrorism as well as to the totalitarian practices of U.S. government at home, and its aggressive foreign policies. Similarly, the limited political horizon in *The Road* precludes the possibility of a future other than the entropy envisaged in the nightmarish descriptions of the end of the world. The logic of narrative in the McCarthy novel, in particular, strives to elude the contradictions and inconsistencies implicit in its ideological frame, while the dissonant perspectives in *Falling Man* are ultimately contained in the narrative return to the site of trauma. I hope my reading of these two texts in what follows will work towards the uncovering of what Jameson has termed "the political unconscious" in these texts in an attempt to make manifest the silences, rifts and dissonances that have remained unrealized in their surface unity.[2]

NOTES to INTRODUCTION

[1] Giovanna Borradori, *Philosophy in a Time of Terror: Dialogues with Jürgen Habermas and Jacques Derrida*, The University of Chicago Press, Chicago, 2003, 28. [italics mine]

[2] Fredric Jameson, *The Political Unconscious: Narrative as a Socially Symbolic Act*, Routledge, London, 2002.

PART I

· ·

"WHAT COMES AFTER AMERICA?": DON DELILLO'S *FALLING MAN*

Strangely, the foreigner lives within us: he is the hidden face of our identity, the space that wrecks our abode, the time in which understanding and affinity founder.
—Kristeva, *Strangers to Ourselves*

Don DeLillo's fourteenth novel *Falling Man* which came out in 2007, six years after the terrorist attacks on the World Trade Center in Manhattan, registers both the immediate impact of the traumatic event on individuals and reflects on the consequent mood of insecurity and disintegration in the years that followed.[1] The falling man of the title suggests, accordingly, both the actual victims who, entrapped in the burning towers, fell to their death on September 11, 2001, and the metaphorical fall experienced by the novel's several characters into a post/9/11 world. The novel spans a period of three years following the attacks with focus on the quotidian life experiences of New Yorkers faced with an uncertain, and not at all promising, future. DeLillo's keenly expected, yet indifferently received novel draws on the stock list of material commonly used in post-9/11 fiction—trauma, loss, death, memory, family, the end of the American holiday from history, the role of the media in the manipulation of public consciousness, and the state's domestic and foreign policies. Arguably unoriginal in terms of its literary themes, however, *Falling Man* merits attention for the aesthetic insights it offers into the experience of trauma as well as for its formal organization and stylistic intricacies that cast

1

doubt on the prevalent assumptions underlying the 9/11 public discourse contingent on the instrumentalisation of trauma.

The novel's plot can be briefly summarized as follows:

Keith Neudecker, a lawyer working for a real estate company in the north tower at World Trade Center, survives the terrorist attacks on September 11, and wanders injured and confused in the streets of lower Manhattan. His colleague Rumsey has died in his arms during the attacks. Keith's mind registers glimpses of the scene of the disaster as he leaves the site in a state of shock. He is given a lift by an electrician, and ends up, unthinkingly, in his estranged wife's apartment. Lianne takes him to the hospital where he is treated for his injuries. Keith and Lianne have been married for eight years, but were separated a year and a half ago. Keith lived in an apartment in lower Manhattan during the separation, and played poker weekly with his friends as a social pastime. Lianne, a free-lance editor of academic books, lived in her uptown apartment with their seven-year-old son Justin, and was involved in voluntary work for Alzheimer patients. Lianne's father had suffered from Alzheimer's, too, and committed suicide to escape senile dementia. Lianne is worried over her genetic disposition, and has medical tests regularly to detect the possible signs of the disease. The poker nights end after the attacks—two players were killed, one was badly injured—but Lianne's weekly writing sessions with Alzheimer patients in East Harlem continue. Following their reunion in the aftermath of the event, Keith and Lianne try to restore their marriage and live as a family again, their attempted reconciliation providing the scene for staging the effects of trauma. Keith has left the tower carrying a briefcase he has unwittingly salvaged; he discovers the identity of the owner, a black woman named Florence Givens, whom he visits in order to return the briefcase. Keith and Florence are involved in an affair which does not last longer than a couple of weeks. They share memories of the event and talk about their lives in an effort to overcome the trauma. Keith takes up another job, briefly, similar to the one he had before the attacks. The impact of the traumatic event is still palpable in the life of the New Yorkers: Lianne assaults a neighbor whom she associates with the terrorists because of the music she hears coming from her apartment on a lower floor. Their son Justin keeps searching the sky for more airplanes that he believes will be sent by a mysterious terrorist named "Bill Lawton". A performance artist named David Janiak begins to appear in the streets enacting the fall of the 9/11 victims from the World Trade Center towers, stirring feelings of rage and repulsion. The Neudeckers' family circle includes Lianne's mother Nina Bartos, a distinguished professor of art history, and her long-time lover Martin Ridnour, aka Ernst Hechinger, a German art dealer who was once associated with European leftist activism. Nina and Martin are gradually driven apart by their strongly opposing views of the events of 9/11. Two and a half years later, Nina dies. The Neudeckers' marriage, too, fails eventually. Keith resumes his interest in poker in a different form, and ends up as a competitive, compulsive poker player in the world of international poker tournaments while Lianne turns to religion in order to be able to continue her life with her son.

In a parallel narrative to the story of the New Yorkers, *Falling Man* tells the story of a terrorist called Hammad who is in the plane that hits the north tower on September 11, 2001, where Keith is sitting at his desk. Related in the form of relatively much shorter episodes from the hijacker's life ending in his suicidal-murderous act on the eventful day, Hammad's story follows him from Hamburg to Florida, and finally to New York, with occasional flashbacks of memory that provide glimpses of his life at a terrorist training camp in Afghanistan. As a student studying mechanical drawing at a technical school in Hamburg where he lives in dire conditions, Hammad mixes with a group of radical Islamists and is soon recruited by Amir—Mohammad Atta—to take part in the planned attacks on U.S. targets. After his training in Afghanistan, Hammad moves, with Amir and others, to Florida to attend flight simulation lessons. In spite of his worldly appetites and his doubts about the justification of their planned act, he is finally overwhelmed by Amir's unwavering steadfastness, and commits himself fully to his mission. Hammad's narrative ends with an account of his last minutes on board the plane that crosses through the Hudson corridor and strikes the north tower where Keith Neudecker is at his desk. The two narrative lines merge at the novel's conclusion with a return to the moment that has initiated the action of the novel.

The novel consists of three parts each of which has as its title a name associated with varying degrees of terror: "Bill Lawton" is a phantom terrorist invented by children who have misheard the name Bin Laden; "Ernst Hechinger" turns out to be the birth name of Martin Ridnour, Nina's lover, who used to be a member of the German anarchist group Kommune 1, and was probably associated with the Baader-Meinhoff Gang of 1960s; and finally "David Janiak" is the performance artist publicly known as the "Falling Man" who performs terror-inducing staged falls in public places in New York, evoking the 9/11 victims who fell to their death from the towers. Each part contains passages indicated by numbers—a total of 14 passages—dealing with the New Yorkers' predicament spread over three years in the aftermath of 9/11. The chapters providing sketchy accounts of the experiences of the novel's terrorist, Hammad, appear at the end of each part to the effect that each of the three major parts of the novel includes some part of the terrorist's story.

The narrative begins in the immediate aftermath of the event with Keith Neudecker, initially unnamed, walking out of the North Tower which has been hit by one of the suicide planes. This and the later life experiences of Keith and other people around him take place in the present time of the narrative which belongs in a post-9/11 temporality—"These are the days after" (138)—the "after" of the attacks, with scattered flashbacks to their past lives. The chapters titled "On Marienstrasse" and "In Nokomis" coming at the end of the first and second parts tell about Hammad's pre-9/11 life in Germany and the States respectively, and constitute the discursive "before" in the narrative. In the last chapter titled "In the Hudson Corridor", in which Hammad emerges as one of the hijackers in the plane that hits the North Tower, the narrative comes full circle to a discursive "now", which is 9/11. Thus, at the conclusion of the novel Hammad and Keith are brought onto the same temporality, the "now" of 9/11, at the very moment when Hammad's plane hits the North Tower where Keith works as a lawyer for a real estate company. Thus "the two chronologies, that are both from time to time interrupted by flashbacks that remain within their respective worlds," as Sven Cvek observes, "collapse into the disaster that engenders the discursive "now" of the novel".[2] The structuring of temporal planes whereby the chronological beginning—9/11—comes at the end of the novel serves for a textual re-enactment of the original trauma while the circular movement of the narrative, in its refusal of easy closure, underscores the novel's pessimism concerning the future. The progress of history related in the discursive "after" of the narrative is brought to a halt to the effect that "any defined notion of future is occluded by the return of the catastrophic event at the end of the novel."[3]

It is worth noting that *Falling Man* was not written as an immediate and direct reaction to the terrorist attacks on 9/11—in fact DeLillo, originally "didn't ever want to write a novel about 9/11" as he told in an interview he gave to *Die Zeit* magazine on 11 October 2007. In the same interview, DeLillo said he started to work on *Falling Man* "the day after George W. Bush's re-election in 2004" because he "needed an internal counterweight":

> We find ourselves in a strange state. After 9/11, the American people stood behind their government, there were no protests against the military action in Afghanistan, and at first there was no criticism of the Iraq war. And even today, although public opinion in polls has tipped over, one does not sense a public attitude of protest which could even remotely remind you of how it was during the Viet Nam war. As one of the characters in *Falling Man* puts it, I feel this way too: I don't know America anymore.[4]

Although *Falling Man* does not explicitly refer to the post-9/11 "War on Terror" the impact of the rhetoric is visible throughout the novel in the allusions to the increase in security measures and the spreading fear and distrust of the Eastern other with the subsequent anxiety experienced by people of Middle-East origins as well as the U.S. military intervention in Afghanistan and Iraq. The post-9/11 New York resembles "a city somewhere else, under permanent siege (25); upon her arrival in New York after the attacks, Nina cannot help "commenting on the [guard]man's uniform, the question of jungle camouflage in midtown Manhattan" (34). Keith has to pass through several check points over and over again, showing the cops "his proof of address and picture ID" (24) to get to his apartment in lower Manhattan, and in order to be allowed access into the district, resorts to a story he fabricates about his children worrying over their cats left in the apartment. DeLillo's portrayal of the city in the immediate aftermath of the attacks in the novel is largely drawn from his observations in his essay titled "In the Ruins of the Future: Reflections on Terror and Loss in the Shadow of September", published only two months after the attacks:

> Six days after the attacks, the territory below Canal Street is hedged with barricades. There are few civilians in the street. Police at some checkpoints, troops wearing camouflage gear and gas masks at others, and a pair of state troopers in conversation, and 10 burly men striding east in hard hats, work pants and NYPD jackets. A shop owner tries to talk a cop into letting him enter his place of business. He is a small elderly man with a Jewish accent, but there is no relief today. Garbage bags are everywhere in high, broad stacks. The area is bedraggled and third-worldish, with an air of permanent emergency, everything surfaced in ash.[5]

In the novel the fear of possible acts of terrorism is spread through official warnings—"Please report any suspicious behavior or unattended packages" (127). As Keith observes it is "difficult to find a taxi in New York where every cabdriver is named Mohammad" (28). Omar H., one of the participants in Lianne's storyline sessions with the Alzheimer patients, is "nervous" about writing "about the planes," (31) and says he "was afraid to go out on the streets in the days after" (61). The novel's repeated allusions to the repressive policies of the state apparatus include the trial of a lawyer "an American woman," "accused of aiding the cause of terrorism," because she "was associated with a radical Muslim cleric who was serving a life sentence for terrorist activity" (217).[6] The media-supported aggressive U.S. foreign politics is pointed through the allusions to the war launched on Afghanistan—"a correspondent in a desolate landscape, Afghanistan or Pakistan, pointed over his shoulder to mountains in the distance," (131) and the protests against the war on Iraq, watched by "police helicopters [going] beating overhead," and policemen on the grounds ready to "detain the overcommitted and uncontrollable" (181).

The subjection of the American public to the divisive rhetoric of "Us and Them" and to the media bombardment of news and images manufacturing fear and hatred is best illustrated in the portrayal of Lianne, Keith's wife. Apparently a suggestible person, and "curious about the wrong things," (12) Lianne has always yearned "to be other people" (105), and seems to lack self-confidence to shape her own views independently. She fully submits herself to the media coverage of 9/11, reading every bit of news, commentaries and the victims' obituaries in the papers "every one that was printed," because "not to read them, every one, was an offense, a violation of responsibility and trust" (106). In the days following the attacks, she is disturbed by the words "Revolt of Islam" on the face of a postcard with a reproduction of the cover of the first edition of Shelley's poem. The postcard, she understands, was sent prior to the event by her friend Carol staying in Rome, but still makes her nervous: "It was a matter of simple coincidence, or not so simple, that a card might arrive at this particular time bearing the title of that specific book" (8). When later she meets Carol in New York, Lianne cannot help noticing the silk blouse her friend is wearing, her thoughts revealing a heightened awareness of otherness: "The blouse she was wearing belonged to another body type, another skin color, a knockoff of a Persian or Moroccan robe" (140). An editor of academic books with degrees "that were meant to take her into deeper scholarship, into serious work in languages or art history," (46) Lianne cannot distinguish between the cultural specifities of Iran and Morocco, dumping them both into the reductive categories of "another body type, another skin color." She has travelled through Europe and Middle East in the past, but only as a tourist, and without "determined inquiry into beliefs, institutions, languages, art," as her mother Nina puts it. (46)

This is made most explicit in her violent encounter with her neighbor who keeps playing a music which sounds "Middle Eastern, North African," and resembles "Bedouin songs [. . .] or Sufi dances" (67). She is quick to condemn the neighbor's music "located in Islamic tradition," (67) "as a certain form of political and religious statement," for being too offensive to be played "now of all times" (69). Her description of the same music—"solo lute from Turkey or Egypt or Kurdistan" (120)—shows her ignorance of other cultures she easily associates with terrorism. The neighbor's name is Elena, so Lianne thinks "maybe Elena [is] Greek," (67) and her dog's name Marko—"He spells his name with a *k*" (124)—has some significance big enough to justify her suspicions about the woman who plays "this particular music at this highly sensitive time" (68). The Greek Elena does not own but rent the apartment she lives in "like people in the Middle Ages" (68). Her otherness makes her one of those people "who think alike, talk alike, eat the same food at the same time [. . .] say the same prayers, word for word, in the same prayer stance, day and night, following the arc of sun moon" (68). Lianne's reductive view of the Eastern other is ironic given that she is currently editing a book on ancient alphabets, and the forms writing took throughout the ages—"pictograms, hieroglyphics, cuneiform"—in civilizations as old as the "Sumerians, Assyrians, so on" (149). As Kauffman points, "[a]lthough DeLillo does not belabor the point, all these forms took root throughout the Middle East—ancient Egyptian, Sumerian, Assyrian, Mesopotamian cultures—the very region the U.S. begins bombing by *Falling Man*'s conclusion."[7] Interestingly, the free association of her thoughts links her memory of a sign she has once seen on a shop window in Santa Fe for an "ethnic shampoo," (23) to the book she is working on, whose author is "a Bulgarian writing in English" (22). The Bulgarian author's "meticulous decipherments" of ancient writings," however, are likely to be lost on Lianne, for his emendations on his text "typed on an old manual machine," are written in "a deeply soulful and unreadable script" (23). Lianne's prejudices conflating different cultures and religious practices become all the more ironic when we are later told that she was herself conceived in Greece. Her parents had met "on a small island in the northeast Aegean where Jack [her father] had designed a cluster of white stucco dwellings for an artists' retreat," and "here, on a hard cot, on a second visit, was where Lianne was conceived," with "music floating up from the waterfront, sort of Greek-Oriental" (130).

DeLillo's depiction of the scene in which Lianne goes to her neighbor's door and assaults her defamiliarizes violence in its detailed account of the act. The arrogance is initially verbal: "The whole city is ultrasensitive right now. Where have you been hiding?" (120). When Elena, "radiating a lifetime of alertness to insult," tries to dismiss her provocative remarks Lianne gets physically violent and "twist[s] her open hand in Elena's face, under the left eye, and push[es] her back into the entranceway," and finally "mash[es] the hand into the eye" (120). An hour later when she recounts the incident to Keith, Lianne unwittingly points to the source of her "totally crazy" act: "Thoughts I can't identify, thoughts I can't claim as mine" (124-5). DeLillo's narration repeatedly calls attention to the way the media coverage of 9/11 impacts on Lianne: "I read newspapers. I put my head in the pages and get angry and crazy" (42). Lianne's line of thinking overlaps with the rhetoric of self-righteous innocence which is used to justify the use of violence on people who are indiscriminately designated as the guilty others. In Lianne's violent confrontation with Elena, one can read the hint directed at the mechanisms by means of which public consent to even the most unjustifiable acts of violence—like the war on Afghanistan and Iraq—can be easily manufactured. Although incomparable in scale and outcome to the violence of the suicide attacks, Lianne's act, too, is resentment-motivated. It may be argued that her violence comes as a reaction to the violence of 9/11, and therefore makes it more forgivable. However, at the receiving end of Lianne's assault is someone who has nothing to do with the terrorists, her only fault being "maybe Greek" and the music she plays.

This self-righteous reasoning is partially accountable for the rage that terror exploits and exposes, and is a symptom of the logic of "War on Terror"; "This is retaliation in itself," thinks Lianne as she contemplates that the most appropriate action in response to Elena's "offense" is to "adopt a posture of fake civility, as a tactic, a means of answering one offense with another" (68). In DeLillo's choice of words one can detect a problematisation of the "fight against the axis of evil" which killed, indiscriminately, thousands of people in Afghanistan and Iraq in retaliation for the terrorist attacks, and in the name of civilization: "fake civility" as "a means of answering one offense with another" (68). The elaborate account of Lianne's thoughts and act puts into question the theses in support of reciprocatory violence while simultaneously demonstrating the impact of ideology on the individual subject who gives unquestioning consent to the politics of hegemonic globalism.

In his "Ruins" essay written long before the appearance of *Falling Man*, DeLillo describes the event that was "so vast and terrible that it was outside imagining even as it happened."[8] DeLillo insists on the need for a counternarrative to resist the totalizing discourses of terrorism and politics both of which rely on the power of the media to monopolize public opinion. What we need, he asserts, is "the smaller objects and more marginal stories sifted in the ruins of the day" in order to "set against the massive spectacle that continues to seem unmanageable, too powerful a thing to set into our frame of practiced response."[9]

In *Falling Man*, DeLillo attempts to explore the possibilities for the kind of counternarrative that would resist the totalizing narrative of terrorism and the official story summoned by U.S. politicians and media pundits in the aftermath of 9/11. Considering DeLillo's previous preoccupation with contemporary American culture and its global impacts, American politics and international terrorism, and the role of the media in the production and manipulation of social consciousness in novels such as *Libra*, *Underworld*, *Mao II*, and *Cosmopolis*, his apparent reluctance, in *Falling Man*, to engage directly with the historical and the political is intriguing. Evidenced by the purposive evasion of words directly referring to the terrorist attacks on 9/11 (it is always "the planes" in the novel and words like "9/11", "Al-Qaeda", and "War on Terror" are conspicuously omitted; the name "Bin Laden" appears once as does Mohammad Atta's full name who goes in the narrative by his middle name "Amir") the exclusion of the directly political draws attention to the process whereby the recovery from trauma is impeded by the self-deceptive rhetoric of "Us and Them." For the "Us and Them" story—a nostalgic remnant of Cold War rhetoric on which the U.S. Administration seems to be fixated—is the narrative which, DeLillo asserts "ends in the rubble."[10] The focus on the "more marginal stories" that are set against the narratives of terrorism and hegemonic politics in *Falling Man* attests to the author's professed aim to produce a counter narrative which is "left to us to create."[11] Kauffman argues that DeLillo adopts a deconstructive strategy throughout the text in order to open up a new space in which the possibility arises for a counternarrative:

> In both the essay and *Falling Man*, DeLillo contrasts al Qaeda with America; medieval vengeance with advanced technology; a brotherhood of martyrs with global markets. But he deconstructs the very dichotomies others reinforce. He cites the (over-determined) history of global capitalism's ill effects leading up to September 11: rapid destabilization, displacement of millions of refugees, the vast discrepancy between our wealth and their suffering. [12]

However, although DeLillo touches on the ill effects of globalised capitalism in his essay the authorial voice in the novel refrains from explicitly commenting on them. Unlike the earlier novels' concern with the links between globalization and terrorism, *Falling Man* contains the discussion of political issues within the national body politic. DeLillo has described his 9/11 novel as "an intimate story which is encompassed by a global event."[13] The structuring of the narrative that begins and ends on the day of the attacks seems to be in line with that description—the intimate story of the American characters related in three parts, each marked off with a coda conveying the terrorist's story. Consequently, the structuring of the text that narrates the stories of the Americans and the terrorists separately, taking place in markedly different temporalities appears to be informed by, and to enact, the dominant ideology materialized in the rhetoric of "Us and Them". Notwithstanding, it must be noted that the text is replete with contradictions that work through and ultimately denaturalize the implicated binary oppositions in the discursive practices which shape social consciousness. Beginning with the opening sentence of the novel the unease with boundaries is betrayed: "It was not a street anymore but a world, a time and space of falling ash and near night" (3). The street into which Keith has just walked out of one of the burning towers is reduced to an apocalyptic scene suggested by the collapse of the temporal and spatial coordinates in ashes and in darkness. Yet in another sense the wording suggests that a particular street in lower Manhattan stops being what it is—"not a street anymore but a world"—and is extended into "a world" (3). The expansion is, a few sentences later, modified with the shift from the indefinite article to the definite: "This was the world now" (3). The street is not just encompassed by, but becomes "the world"; it is not simply a metonymic relation which is being evoked here between the local and the global, but the collapse of the boundaries between them. As Cvek maintains: "The novel's opening paragraphs can be seen as marking the moment of a particular expansion, of the "worlding" of local experience: "this," the street, becomes "the world"—the traumatic moment thus marks a point of the US subject's entry into 'world history'". [14] However, the entry into world history comes in the form of a fall: "The world was this as well, figures in windows a thousand feet up, dropping into free space" (4). The novel's first reference to people dropping to their death from the towers both collectivizes the experience of the fall—"figures in windows"—and marks it as an entry into world history—"the world was this as well". Finally, the metaphor of the "Falling Man" suggesting an entry into world history as a fall is implicated in Keith's identification with the falling tower—"That was him coming down, the north tower"—as he hears "the sound of the second fall" (5). The designation of Keith as the subject who falls—"that was him coming down"—compounded by the Biblical resonance of the phrase "the second fall" is indicative of a postlapsarian state of existence—America's entry into history—because as Brauner notes, "the fall of the towers seemed to symbolize the end of an era of American innocence (in the sense of naivety, if not of moral purity)."[15] Significantly, this is the moment when Keith begins "to see things, somehow, differently" (5) in the novel's post-9/11 world where "everything now is measured by after" (138).

While the novel's major thematic concern seems to be the immediate and later impact of the traumatic event manifested in the "intimate story" of Keith Neudecker's family circle, in the narrative treatment of that story a resistance is detectable against the prevalent tendency to reduce the inscription of the "global event" to a narrative which points up the family as the site in which trauma can be overcome. "[W]hile trauma is a fundamental concept for the understanding of the novel," as Cvek observes, "it is important to stress that *Falling Man* also insists on the openness and unfamiliarity of the national historical moment, and consistently refuses to painlessly work through the traumatic event by enclosing it in a definite narrative account."[16] Keith's temporary reunion with Lianne in the immediate aftermath of the attacks reflects on the way DeLillo treats the transposition of political issues on to the domestic sphere. When Keith Neudecker inadvertently finds himself in the doorway to his wife's apartment immediately after his escape from the towers on September 11, 2001, "the intimate story encompassed by a global event" begins to unravel. The resolution of the national drama through a return to an idealized past epitomized by the nuclear family is problematised in the novel as the Neudeckers, already separated a year and a half previously, do not exactly fit into the narrative of the familial idyll destroyed by a hostile other. Furthermore, the family in *Falling Man* is shown to dissipate irrecoverably in the face of the traumatic event, suggesting the inadequacy of the hegemonic cultural tendency displacing national politics on to the intimate sphere.

Keith and Lianne's eight-year marriage has already failed in the past; their post-9/11 union, too, falls short of developing into a gratifying relationship. Lianne sits, "three days after the planes," (8) thinking of "the early times, eight years ago, of the eventual extended grimness called their marriage" (7). Six days after the planes her mother Nina reminds Lianne that "marrying the man was a huge mistake," (11) and warns her against their re-union. In the early days of their marriage, Lianne reminisces, "sex was everywhere" (7), and now, "fifteen days after the planes," sex is "the only interval she'd known in these days and nights that was not forced or distorted" (69). Lianne is content to have "the stranger [she] married in another lifetime" (35) back in her life, and believes "this is where he wanted to be, outside the tide of voices and faces, God and country, sitting alone in still rooms, with those nearby who mattered" (20). Keith, in the past, "used to want to fly out of self-awareness,"(66) and now to him "nothing seem[s] familiar, being here, in a family again," and he feels "strange to himself, or always had" (65). While Lianne believes "he is growing into it, a husbandman," (70) Keith is already involved with another woman, Florence Givens, whose briefcase he has salvaged on the day of the attacks. The routine of family life includes his extra-marital affair, as it did in the past: "There were the walks to and from school, the meals he cooked

[. . .] There was the park, every kind of weather, and there was the woman who lived across the park. But that was another matter, the walk across the park" (66). Keith and Lianne resume their marriage because they both want "contact," (35) and are "ready to sink back into [their] little lives," (75) with the conflicts that led to their separation remaining unresolved. Keith continues to be the reticent man he has always been "who would not submit to [Lianne's] need for probing intimacy" (105). As Lianne finally admits, he had "never felt right," in the kind of middle-class family life typified by "autumn weekends at somebody's country house, leaf-fall and touch football, kids tumbling down grassy slopes," and "it would be impossible now for him to feel any different" (190). And Lianne, herself, is isolated from that life, too: "She hadn't stayed in close touch, and felt no guilt or need" (190). On the rare occasions she goes out, she "[goes] out alone, [does] not stay late" (190).

The family as the hegemonic site of national politics expressed in Lianne's formula for "times like these," when "the family is necessary," to "live through the things that scare us half to death," (214) dissipates in *Falling Man* in the face of the global event, and the treatment of the intimate story encompassed by that event points out the limits of the 9/11 rhetoric composed of formulaic statements on the "national drama". DeLillo, as Duvall writes: "resists the notion of a new American identity based on collective trauma": "We hope that Keith and Lianne will successfully make their marriage work, that this reunification will provide the Shakespearian happy ending that will offer a kind of symbolic healing of the wound of 9/11. This hope, however, is frustrated."[17] In its refusal to provide a closure to the family narrative, the novel "insists on the traumatic monstrosity of the unfinished process of transition, without offering even an approximate vision of a safer future."[18]

Kierkegaard's "the whole of existence frightens me" (118) comes to articulate Lianne's mood of living "in the spirit of what is ever impending" (212). Haunted by the memory of her father who "died by his own hand" (169) to escape senile dementia, and tormented by the inevitable demise of the Alzheimer patients who "approached what was impending [. . .] with a little space remaining, at this point, to stand and watch it happen," (94)

14

Lianne keeps "counting down from one hundred by sevens" (218). She loses her husband to poker, her mother dies, and Martin leaves for good; Lianne "counts down" as the affective communal ties she desperately wants to cling to break in the face of trauma. Her conversion to Christianity towards the end of the novel attests to her wish to disengage from the historical process in the same way as her moment of epiphany that makes her feel "ready to be alone, in reliable calm, she and the kid, the way they were before the planes appeared that day," (236) implies a wished for erasure (or reversal) of history. Yet, as the doctor treating Alzheimer patients has already warned her, "from this point on [. . .] it's all about loss. We're dealing inevitably here with diminishing returns" (60). Keith, on the other hand, responds to the pressure of the historical moment by escaping into the timeless artificiality Las Vegas provides. His suspended fall takes the form of a journey from the collapsing towers to the gambling parlors where he ends up in a kind of arrested life, a life in death. Terry Cheng's joking remark comparing poker players to vampires returning to their coffins before dawn "disguises a deeper truth, which is that Keith has chosen an artificial environment that is anonymous, hermetically sealed, ruled by a strict code. It is a denatured world outside of time (no clocks in casinos)."[19]

Responding to a question concerning the genesis of his 9/11 novel, DeLillo said he initially had in his mind the picture of a "man, walking through the streets of Manhattan after the attack, shrouded in clouds of dust and ash." When he started working on *Falling Man*, he discovered that the picture which had surfaced in his imagination came from a photograph that had appeared in the papers after the attacks, showing "a businessman, in ashes and dust, with a bag in his hand." *Falling Man* originated in DeLillo's musings concerning the story of the man and the bag in his hand:

> I asked myself: *Who is this man? What's his story? And what about the bag he's got?* I tried to answer these questions with the force of my imagination. Suddenly I hit upon the idea that the bag didn't belong to the man at all. Who did it belong to? Why did

he have it with him? I placed myself, like a detective, into my own plot.[20]

The businessman with the bag emerges in the novel as Keith Neudecker, the lawyer, holding a briefcase which does not belong to him but, as he is soon to discover, to a black woman named Florence Givens, another survivor from the towers. The brief case Keith unwittingly salvages during his escape from the burning tower remains briefly in his estranged wife Lianne's apartment before being returned to Florence. The trajectory of the briefcase from Lianne's uptown apartment where the couple live in a semblance of family life to Florence's apartment "just off Amsterdam Avenue," (52) where the two survivors have a brief affair points in the direction of a potential new life—"a new deck"—for Keith Neudecker. Florence Givens "gives" Keith the chance to overcome his traumatic experience by talking "about the tower, going over it again, claustrophobically, the smoke, the fold of bodies," and Keith understands "that they could talk about these things only with each other, in minute and dullest detail, but it would never be dull or too detailed because it was inside them now and because he needed to hear what he'd lost in the tracings of memory" (90-91). With her name "evok[ing] Florence Nightingale, the kindly nurse who ministered to wounded men," Florence ministers to Keith's traumatized soul and "believes Keith saved her life by appearing at her door, because she has no one else to turn to."[21] Florence's description from Keith's perspective intimates her otherness: A "light-skinned black woman," she is "one of those odd embodying of doubtful language and unwavering race," (92) and lives "across the park," (89) indicating class distinctions between the East and West sides of New York. In one sense, then, Florence's briefcase that has landed on Keith's hands on September 11 offers him the possibility of traversing the boundaries of his middle-class existence. As Rowe argues:

[DeLillo] gestures in the direction of Keith's and Florence's cultural, ethnic, and class differences, overlooked briefly as a consequence of a shared, but passing post-traumatic stress. Their undeveloped interlude is strange indeed in the novel, because it is one of the very few times characters in the novel actually cross the boundaries of their small worlds, apart from the framing act of al-Qaeda's attack, in itself a fundamental transgression of realms.[22]

Inside the briefcase salvaged from the World Trade Center's collapsed towers is a compact disc containing a compilation of music from Brazil that has "a buzz and drive, voices in Portuguese rapping, singing, whistling, with guitars and drums behind them, manic saxophones" (92). It is this music which "finally moves Neudecker out of his middle-class propriety"[23] to make love to the woman who seems "to lose herself in the music, eyes closed," and dances "nearly trancelike" (93). Florence, who does not care for her missing cell phone returned in the briefcase—"That thing. I stopped needing it when I didn't have it" (53)—recognizes the true gift they have both been "given": "We all need some Portuguese. We all need to go to Brazil" (93). "Parodying some classic detective plot," as Rowe argues, "DeLillo gives us the "treasure" inside that briefcase as the Brazilian rhythms of Samba or some hybrid musical form, intended to liberate us from the confines of capitalism, print-knowledge, Western Civilization."[24] Florence seems responsive to the intuitively felt possibility of another world the music inspires, whereas Keith's vision remains limited to "a job involving Brazilian investors" (93). As Rowe puts it,

> At some level, DeLillo suggests that these personal failures—whether Keith's inability to hear the Brazilian rhythms Florence so clearly feels or Lianne's reduction of the music Elena plays to "noise" (68-69)—are symptomatic of our national problem and explain in part our susceptibility to terror.[25]

Not surprisingly Keith ends his relationship with Florence, which is tainted by "the sense of ill-matched people" that "was not completely dispelled" (107), and in its stead opts for a stable life he hopes to find in the nuclear family model provided by his wife and son before he finally ends up, practically "homeless", at the poker table. Even deep down in his poker craze, Keith thinks about Florence Givens "in a remote way, like landscape, like thinking of going back to the house where you grew up

17

and walking along the back lanes and across the high meadow, the kind of thing you know you'll never do" (227).

On one of Keith's visits, Florence makes a remark which is ostensibly addressed to Keith but is also a metafictional response to Don DeLillo's question about the bag the man in the picture had with him: "You ask yourself what the story is that goes with the briefcase? I'm the story" (109). The story which is Florence Givens, however, remains unrealized in the text. By the end of the narrative we know that Keith had "never thought of crossing the park again to see her, talk a while, find out how she was doing" (227). In DeLillo's *Falling Man*, the incomplete story of Keith and Florence constitutes a narrative gap pointing at an anxiety concerning the ideological limitations of the discursive frame of the text which is betrayed by the inability of the novel's falling man to think beyond the capitalist paradigm.

The vaguely implied promise of an alternative life outside the confines of capitalism and Western civilization is lost on Keith and he turns his back on Florence. His attempted re-union with his wife cannot survive the traumatic event, either. Far from being the remedy for the working through of trauma, intimate relationships in *Falling Man* falter and eventually come to an end. Nina Bartos grows increasingly estranged from Martin Ridnour, her lover for twenty years as their conflicting views of terrorism drive them apart before Nina dies. Nina's deteriorating health has something to do with her feelings about her involvement with Martin. Lianne believes her mother's "slackness of will was a defeat that had Martin in the middle of it. These were his nineteen, these hijackers, these jihadists, even if only in her mother's mind" (149). Nina sees Martin "only rarely in the last two and a half years of her life" and each hears "news of the other through mutual friends or from Lianne" (191). It is his "guilt by association" that brings the relationship to an end, and after Nina's death Martin becomes "someone displaced or deeply distracted, lost in time" (191). Martin has sold his apartment in New York and reduced his business commitments there, his future in "one city" he does not yet know where, in which he sees himself "trapped" (194). Martin does not "know this America anymore," (193) which "becomes the center of its own shit" (191). In the "empty space where America used to be," (193) familial or communal ties break as "the plots, myths, institutions we once relied on to provide meaning and purpose are suspended."[26] For all the 9/11 public discourse which situates the sphere of the intimate at the core of national polity, *Falling Man* shows that sphere disintegrate drastically: not only are the couples separated and friends avoided, but the sense of community presumed to draw people together around shared feelings and ideas becomes obsolete in the anonymity of the gambling parlors Keith chooses, and transforms into its own dark parody in the emerging community of poker players, who meet "like early Christians in hiding," to play "an underground game," which Terry Cheng compares to "a forbidden religion springing up again" (202-3). In the course of the process of transition in U.S. history in which September 11, 2001 marks the moment of radical change, the characters whose quotidian lives constitute the plot in *Falling Man* bear testimony to the predicament of the American subject who ends up as dislocated, isolated, and subjected to contingency as the terrorists who brought about the fall of the World Trade Center. The emergence of the post-9/11 American subject "leads neither to national consolidation nor imperialist expansion, thus diverging distinctly from the direction American domestic and foreign policy took in response to the 9/11 attacks," in DeLillo's novel which, in effect, "stages the fundamental emptiness of such a traumatic emergence of subjectivity: instead of a renewed national body and a reconstituted community, the novel offers a vision of arrested life in a state of emergency."[27]

In his "Ruins" essay, DeLillo situates the event in the process of globalization that has been going on for decades and proceeds to juxtapose the narrative of the West and that of terrorism:

> In the past decade the surge of capital markets has dominated discourse and shaped global consciousness. Multinational corporations have come to seem more vital and influential than governments. [. . .] Terror's response is a narrative that has been developing over years, only now becoming inescapable. It is our lives and minds that are occupied now.[28]

DeLillo goes on to expound on the way "the event has changed the grain of the most routine moment," to the effect that "[w]e may find that the ruin of the towers is implicit in other things": "The new Palm Pilot at a fingertip's reach, the stretch limousine parked outside the hotel, the midtown skyscraper under construction, carrying the name of a major investment bank—all haunted in a way by what has happened, less assured in their authority, in the prerogatives they offer."[29]

In the novel the terrorist narrative is voiced chiefly by Amir—"His full name was Mohamed Mohamed el-Amir el-Sayed Atta" (80)—who is the leader of the hijackers. In the discussions led by Amir, "There was the feeling of lost history. They were too long in isolation. This is what they talked about, being crowded out by other cultures, other futures, the all-enfolding will of capital market and foreign policies" (80). And the jihadist outlook is inscribed in his version of Islam which "is the world outside the prayer room as well as the *surahs* in the Koran, [. . .] the struggle against the enemy, near and far, Jews first, for all things unjust and hateful, and then the Americans" (80). The terrorist paradigm consisting of a mixture of an anti-capitalist position and a distorted version of Islam bent on destruction constitutive of the jihadist outlook that justifies the infliction of violence on the innocent is also echoed in Amir's words: "The others exist only to the degree that they fill the role we have designed for them. This is their function as others. Those who will die have no claim to their lives outside useful fact of their dying" (176).

DeLillo's stereotyped account of Islamic fundamentalism represented by Amir—the representative of pure evil—is partly counterbalanced by his portrayal of Hammad, his fictional terrorist, in more human terms who, unlike Amir, displays signs of self-doubt concerning his position in the opposition between the two worlds. In contrast with the demonization of Amir, manifested in his aberrant denial of the "Western" way of life and his abstinence from bodily pleasures, episodes from Hammad's pre-9/11 life show his indulgence in sex and over-eating, for which he is, indeed, harshly criticized by Amir. At one point in the narrative he even comes close to realizing the tenuity of the boundaries separating the two worlds. Driving in the streets of Nokomis one day, Hammad sees a group of young people "maybe college kids, boys and girls," crammed in a car, "laughing and smoking": "How easy would it be for him to walk out of his car and into theirs? Open the door with the car in motion and walk across the roadway to the other car, walk on air, and open the door of the other car and get in" (172). Nor does DeLillo's terrorist Hammad, possess signs of an intellectual depth to provide a rationale for terrorism; rather his shallowness is implied in his admiration for Amir's arguments which sound less political or philosophical than dogmatic. The fellow Muslims who secretly meet in the run-down flat on Marienstrasse in Hamburg appear to be bonded by a perceived threat against Islam—"they knew that Islam was under attack," (83) and a crude anti-Semitism—accusing Jews even for building thin walls and misshaped toilets (79)—that surface during their conversations, and Hammad's choice seems to be driven by a desire to belong in that community: "He was becoming one of them now, learning to look like them and think like them. This was inseparable from jihad. He prayed with them to be with them. They were becoming total brothers" (83).

DeLillo's analysis of the religious and political motives and the personal psychologies of the hijackers is conspicuously brief (only 22 of the novel's 246 pages deal with the terrorist' story), and his probing into the claims and theories of terrorism remains relatively limited in comparison to his lengthy elaborations in the earlier novels. Rowe argues that the trivialization of the terrorists in the novel shifts the attention from the terrorist claims to the causes of terror:

> DeLillo trivializes the terrorists by minimizing the attention he pays to them in the novel, reinforcing his arguments in *Underworld* (1997) and *Cosmopolis* (2003) that first world, hypercapitalist nations, especially the United States, have created their own antagonists in al-Qaeda and any other "terror" (domestic or foreign) we might experience in our postmodern condition. [. . .] There is no difference between the home-grown American assassin, Lee Harvey Oswald [DeLillo's terrorist in *Libra*] and the imported terrorists of al-Qaeda: terror is the inevitable by-product of a system built

upon unstable master-servant relations that inevitably prompt the servant's rebellion.[30]

The "master-servant relations that inevitably prompt the servant's rebellion" are hardly, if at all, explored in the novel except in the clichés voiced by Amir, who is more demonized than trivialized in the depictions of his monstrous abnormality. However, there exist in the text linguistic and stylistic intricacies that subtly suggest a conception of terrorism integral to the system. That the new form of terrorism in our postmodern condition is a product of globalization itself is subtly implied in the name "Bill Lawton". The explanation for the name which appears as the title of the first part is not provided until page 37 in the text. In the days following the attacks, Keith and Lianne's eight-year-old son Justin begins to spend time with his friends, "the siblings", in their apartment on the twenty-seventh floor of a tall building where they "sort of conspire," and "talk in code" (17). It turns out that they are "searching the skies" (71) with binoculars "for more planes," "waiting for it to happen again" (72). The siblings' mother tells Lianne that the children keep talking about a man named Bill Lawton who, they, believe is the mastermind behind the attacks. The name, it turns out, was invented by the younger sibling, who misheard Bin Laden's name "from television or school or somewhere," and "never adjusted his original sense of what he was hearing" (73). Bill Lawton grows into a myth in the children's imagination, parodying the myth created in public discourse around the figure of al-Qaeda leader Bin Laden: "Bill Lawton has a long beard. He wears a long robe. [. . .] He flies jet planes and speaks thirteen languages but not English except to his wives. [. . .] He has the power to poison what we eat but only certain foods", and he goes "everywhere in his bare feet" (74). Justin develops a habit of talking in monosyllables, which, his mother thinks, sounds "totalitarian," (66) and later the kid discloses that "Bill Lawton talks in monosyllables," and "says things that nobody knows but the Siblings and me" (101-2). DeLillo's emphasis on the phantom American terrorist can be seen to implicate the "American" origins of Bin Laden: Bill Lawton as the domesticated twin of Bin Laden is suggestive of the U.S. involvement in the creation of the actual terrorist Osama Bin Laden as an actor in its cold war with the Soviet Union during the Soviet invasion of Afghanistan in 1980s. In *Falling Man*, Bin Laden's name is mentioned only once, the name Bill Lawton is a secret the children are not supposed to disclose to their parents, and the parents refrain from mentioning it. On realizing the association between the two names, Lianne thinks "that some important meaning might be located in the soundings of the boy's small error," and looks at her husband, "searching for his concurrence, for something she might use to secure her free-floating awe" (73-4). In particular, the difficulty Lianne has remembering the name, and her initial blindness to its obvious association signals the mechanisms of repression—loss of memory is ironically Lianne's obsessive concern—as well as the careful efforts in the 9/11 rhetoric summoned by the government and the media to erase from public memory the facts concerning the U.S involvement in the history of al-Qaeda and Bin Laden.

Bin Laden is, in a sense, a "home grown" terrorist, and although the novel's formal structure draws a thick line between the Americans and the terrorists, the text includes disruptive moments that cut through the divide separating "Us" from "Them". Reading the first part of the novel titled "Bill Lawton," the reader is led into the assumption that the character who has just walked out of one of the burning towers is the eponymous Bill Lawton. Keith's name does not appear until we are nine pages into the novel (three days after the attacks in the narrative's temporal progress) when, in a conversation between Lianne and her mother Nina, it is finally, if still vaguely, revealed that the "He" of the first sequence portraying the minutes after the attacks was Keith. Keith Neudecker—his surname is provided towards the end of the text—is not the phantom Anglo twin of Bin Laden after all, but his professional occupation in "law" rings in the name "Lawton". Law, by definition, involves conformity with laws and rules defined by a governing authority challenged by the twins Lawton/Laden.

Moreover, there are subtle implications in the text about Keith's character that bring him close to a certain perception of terrorists. He is described as a "reticent" man who "gives the impression there's something deeper than hiking and skiing or playing cards" (9-10). Later in the text Hamad's face in the newspaper will seem to Lianne "taut, with hard eyes that seemed too knowing to belong to a face on a driver's license" (19). The terrorist Hammad "thought all his life that some unnamed energy was sealed in his body, too tight to be released" (79). Lianne remembers Keith returning home, night after night not long before their separation, unable to "put into words whatever it was that lay there" and "ready to break up a table and burn it so he could take out his dick and piss on the flames" (104). Nina thinks Keith makes Lianne "feel dangerously alive" and, if he painted or wrote poetry "[he]'d be the raging artist. He'd be allowed to behave unspeakably" (12). Actually, Keith who "used to want more of the world than there was time and means to acquire" (128) was an acting student once, he later tells his fellow survivor/lover Florence. He, too, has wandered aimlessly for a while before he eventually ended up in the law school—"What else? Where else?" (89). The options in life seem limited equally for Keith and Hammad, and both men's lives appear to be predestined by a metaphysical contingency beyond their control.

DeLillo's metaphor for the "terrorist within" is the medical term "organic shrapnel". The doctor in the examining room extracting small fragments of glass embedded in Keith's face during the attacks tells him that the survivors of suicide bombings may develop bumps which are caused by tiny fragments of the suicide bomber's body:

> The bomber is blown to bits, literally bits and pieces, and fragments of flesh and bone come flying outward with such force and velocity that they get wedged, they get trapped in the body of anyone who's in striking range. [. . .] Then, months later, they find these little, like, pellets of flesh, human flesh that got driven into the skin. They call this organic shrapnel. (16)

Almost all of DeLillo's characters appear to be inflicted with organic shrapnel, whether in the form of post-traumatic symptoms they display or in their actions—before or after 9/11—which betray traits attributable to the terrorist other. From Keith's later fanatical commitment to poker, to Lianne's violent assault at her Greek neighbor, to Justin's ties he thinks he has with his imagined terrorist, terror, which DeLillo in his "Ruins" essay sees occupying "*our* lives and minds," becomes increasingly manifest as if the organic shrapnel threatens to overgrow the people it has landed on.

It is, nonetheless, through the character of Martin Ridnour, Nina's twenty-year-long lover, that DeLillo most succinctly introduces the "terrorist within" whose portrayal in the novel subverts, in more than one way, the binary opposition of "Us" and "Them". In the "Ruins" essay DeLillo cannot but express astonishment at how the terrorist "planted in a Florida town, pushing his supermarket trolley, nodding to his neighbor," has lived "years here, waiting, taking flying lessons, making the routine gestures of community and home, the credit card, the bank account, the post-office box."[31] The terrorist's propensity for disguise, his double-life, is a source of constant paranoid fear and distrust of the other who is defined, in the post-9/11 world, broadly as Middle Eastern or Muslim. In *Falling Man* Lianne's paranoia finds its target in Elena who "was either an office manager or a restaurant manager [. . .] and who knew what else," (69) pointing at the possibility of her double identity as a terrorist in disguise. In Martin's case, too, it is his double identity that leads to speculation about his mysterious past; born Ernst Hechinger, he has changed his name to Martin Ridnour, for reasons that remain unknown—"Maybe he killed someone," Lianne speculates (147). However, Martin's presence in the novel as a Westerner—he is a German expatriate—and an ex-anarchist who was probably once involved in the European terrorism of 1960s serves to hollow out the contemporary identification of terror with the Middle East and Islam.[32] Nina knows he was a member of Kommune 1, a collective demonstrating against the German state in the late 1960s: "First they threw eggs. Then they set off bombs. After that I'm not sure what he did. I think he was in Italy for a while, in the turmoil, when the Red Brigades were active. But I don't know" (146). Nina also suspects "he sometimes dealt in stolen art," in his early years as an art dealer. Martin's present life, too, seems to be shrouded in secrecy: he is always "somewhere in Europe," travelling "from a distant city on [his] way to another distant city", neither of which "has shape or form" (42). A "shapeless" man by his own definition, Martin Ridnour is "an art dealer, a collector, an investor perhaps," and Lianne is not sure "what he [does] exactly or how he [does] it," but suspects that he speculates in art "for large profit" (42). He has been with Nina for twenty years, but "not continuously," and "he has a wife," who is "somewhere else too" (145).

With the emphasis placed on his mysterious past suggesting links with the Baader-Meinhoff Gang and the Red Brigades, Martin Ridnour's presence in the novel provides an uncanny link with the jihadists: in his Berlin apartment he keeps a wanted poster of nineteen German terrorists of the early nineteen seventies. "Nineteen names and faces" belonging to people "wanted for murder, bombings, bank robberies," (147) immediately recall the nineteen hijackers whose photographs appeared in papers in the days following September 11. Nina believes that Martin "thinks these people, these jihadists, [. . .] have something in common with the radicals of the sixties and seventies": "He thinks they're all part of the same classical pattern. They have their theorists. They have their visions of world brotherhood" (147).

The positioning of the part titled "Ernst Hechinger" at the centre of the text reinforces the centrality of Martin's position in the narrative as the terrorist within, acting as an intermediary between the divisive categories of "Us" (American) and "Them" (the terrorist Other). "Maybe he was a terrorist but he was one of ours," Lianne thinks when she sees Martin for the last time after her mother's funeral service: "and the thought chilled her, shamed her—one of ours, which meant godless, Western, white" (195). Ernst Hechinger/Martin Ridnour functions as an organic shrapnel located at the centre of DeLillo's novel which reiterates, in its formal structure and temporal organization, the binary oppositions between West/Modern/ and East/Pre-modern on which the 9/11 public discourse depends, and manifests itself in the growing rupture in Nina and Martin's relationship.

In his discussions with Nina, Martin insists on contextualizing terror in terms of a long history of "human grievance against others, every force of history that places people in conflict," involving "lost lands, failed states, foreign intervention, money, empire, oil, the narcissistic heart of the West," as opposed to his lover's presupposition of primitive urges—"whatever blind force, or blunt force, or violent need"—at the roots of terrorism, which is like "a virus" that "reproduces itself outside history" (112-3).

Nina's conflict with Martin "highlights the contradictions between America's self-image and its image in the eyes of the world. Where she sees civilization, he sees brute force—police, prisons, and the military."[33] For Nina Bartos, "It's not the history of Western interference that pulls down these societies. It's their history, their mentality. They live in a closed world of choice, of necessity. They haven't advanced because they haven't wanted to or tried to" (47). In contrast to Martin's interpretation of the 9/11 attacks in terms of historical, economic and social processes Nina Bartos insists the terrorists attack out of "sheer panic": "There are no goals they can hope to achieve. They are not liberating a people or casting out a dictator" (46). Martin thinks the terrorists aim at visibility: "First they kill you, then you try to understand them. Maybe, eventually, you'll learn their names. But they have to kill you first" (113). Nina's views refer back to a pre-globalist paradigm in which social antagonisms were more clearly perceptible and the aims of anti-establishment movements were defined in terms of seizing state power. Martin who was once a participant in this Western-originated form of leftist activism reframes the opposition within the context of globalization: "One side has the capital, the labor, the technology, the armies, the agencies, the cities, the laws, the police and the prisons. The other side has a few man willing to die" (47).

In "The Violence of the Global," Baudrillard notes that "current terrorism is not a descendant of a traditional history of anarchy, nihilism and fanaticism."[34] The paradigmatic shift marked by the transition from the "universal" to the "global" has resulted in a situation whereby "the central gives way not to the local but to the dislocated."[35] Thus,

> [C]onfronted on the one hand with a global order to which there is no alternative, and, on the other, with singularities drifting off on their own or rising up against the system, the concepts of freedom, democracy and human rights cut a very pale figure, being merely the ghosts of a vanished universal[36]

In "the virtual space of the global," Baudrillard goes on to argue, the "dialectical tension and critical movement which found their form in historical and revolutionary violence" are replaced by, the violence of the global: the supremacy of positivity alone and of technical efficiency, total organization, integral circulation, the equivalence of all exchanges," bringing about "the end of the role of the intellectual, bound up with the Enlightenment and the Universal—and also the end of the activist, who was linked to contradictions and historical violence.[37]

In *Falling Man*, the universal intellectual who speaks from within the discursive frame of Enlightenment thought is represented by Nina, the distinguished scholar of arts, who professes her unwavering loyalty to the Judeo-Christian tradition—"I want to sit in my armchair and read my Europeans" (34). The image, evoked in the text, of the old woman whose field of activity is limited to no more than sitting and reading is suggestive of the retreat of the "enlightened" intellectual Baudrillard refers to. Indeed, Nina dies by the end of the novel, having completed her role on the stage of world history. Similarly, the redundancy of the discourse of the European leftist radicalism of 1960s is underscored in the novel, through the portrayal of Martin who is not an activist anymore, but an aging, chubby man; he has actually become a businessman who would have made a perfect target for the Baader-Meinhoff guerrillas—"Kidnap the bastard. Burn his paintings" (148). In the Morandi paintings, which were once the subject of his Marxist critique of art—"empty, self-involved, bourgeois"—he now sees "the light, or "the money" (145-6). Kommune One, the German activist group with which Martin was associated, was known for its Dadaist-style radical performance acts of social satire.[38] Ernst Hechinger's changed identity into Martin Ridnour testifies to his personal history of transformation from the radical who once engaged in transgressive artistic acts against the system into the art dealer who participates in the system's commercialization of art. It also marks the paradigmatic shift underlying personal histories like Martin's; the occasional "slurred pulse of an earlier consciousness," Lianne detects in Martin just before his disappearance in the novel underlines what Baudrillard calls "the end of the activist" in the old sense of the word.

Compounded by the deliberate absence of an authorial voice, the apparent inability of the text to make sense of 9/11 can be said to draw attention to the impossibility of producing an adequate explanation—and response—to the event from the repertory of simplistic and totalizing narratives which all set the terms of the antagonism as clearly separable and easily identifiable entities. Instead, *Falling Man* makes frequent allusions to the postmodern condition in which the first and the third worlds are no longer reducible to politically or geographically demarcated territories only but are integrated through the processes of mobilization and displacement on a global scale. In New York "every cabdriver" is "named Muhammad" (28), an Iraqi ex-soldier in Saddam's war against Iran continues his life as a baker in Hamburg, where Muslim men from all over the world pray in a mosque "on the second floor of this shabby building with graffiti smeared on the outer walls and a setting of local strolling whores" (77-8). Hammad studies in Germany and attends flight courses in Florida. A Muslim woman in "a black headscarf" (181) hands out leaflets in Manhattan in protest of the war on Iraq (recalling the Muslim woman, in the "Ruins" essay, who prays for the dead after the attacks on her rug pointing at the "Manhattan grid," as "the only locational guide" she needs, "that indicates the direction of Mecca"[39]). On the wall of Nina's apartment near Fifth Avenue, hangs a piece "from Martin's collection," composed of passport photos with inscriptions of "the bearer's status and port of embarkation" from all over the world (141). These faces "looking out of a sepia distance, lost in time," speak of "human ordeal set against the rigor of the state," reminding of "people fleeing, there to here, with darkest hardship pressing the edges of the frame" (141-2). Pointing to a world history in "*Cyrillic, Greek, Chinese*" (142) of displacements imposed by political and economic circumstances, these "aged documents, stamped and faded, history measured in inches," are "also beautiful" (46). Under the hegemony of capitalist exchange even human misery cannot escape commodification; the "deeper meaning than an ocean crossing alone might account for" in the face and eyes of the young woman in one the photos, who looks "Jewish, *Staatsangehörigkeit*," (142) is transplanted onto an aesthetic object which is prone to the dictates of the global art market represented in the novel by the German dealer Martin Ridnour, who has "an apartment here [in New York], and an office in Basel," and "spend[s] time in Berlin" (42). Historical and cultural differences continue to be politically manipulated but the hegemonic ideology of global capitalism does not discriminate between the identities of individuals whom it interpellates as the consuming subject. In the days following the attacks, Keith Neudecker makes a habit of correcting the misspellings of his name on his mail, but he does not bother to correct the spelling on mail that is "outright third-class indiscriminate throw away advertising matter," for he is aware that "junk mail [is] created for just this reason, to presort the world's identities into one, with his or her name misspelled" (31-2). When the suicide planes hit the towers, "contracts, resumes [. . .] intact snatches of business," (4) float in free space in sad mockery of the global free flow of capital through the World Trade Centre, one of the centers of global hegemony.[40] Keith, unemployed after the attacks is offered a job involving "Brazilian investors," who are "engaged in real-estate transactions in New York" (104). The surge of capital markets that "has dominated discourse and shaped global consciousness," as DeLillo asserts in his "Ruins" essay, knows no national boundaries and cultural differences as "[m]ultinational corporations have come to seem more vital and influential than governments."[41]

The new terrorism which DeLillo defines in his "Ruins" essay as "the global theocratic state, unboundaried and floating"[42] is well at home with late capitalism, making use of credit cards from global banks, of money wired from Dubai, a major global financial centre in the Middle East, and its advanced technology which the terrorists turn against itself as well as its obsession with image and spectacle on which they depend for the colossal impact of their violent act. In the "Ruins" essay DeLillo writes:

> The World Trade towers were not only an emblem of advanced technology but a justification, in a sense, for technology's irresistible will to realize in solid form whatever becomes theoretically allowable. Once defined, every limit must be reached. The tactful sheathing of the towers was intended to reduce the direct threat of such straight-edge enormity, a giantism that eased over the years into something a little more familiar and comfortable, even dependable in a way.

Now a small group of men have literally altered our skyline. We have fallen back in time and space. It is their technology that marks our moments, the small, lethal devices, the remote-control detonators they fashion out of radios, or the larger technology they borrow from us, passenger jets that become manned missiles.

Maybe this is a grim subtext of their enterprise. They see something innately destructive in the nature of technology. It brings death to their customs and beliefs. Use it as what it is, a thing that kills.[43]

DeLillo's Middle-Eastern terrorists in *Mao II*—a novel set in 1980s—were probably the last representatives of the traditional revolutionary left with their faith in the possibility of changing the world and their secular discourse including quotes from Chairman Mao.[44] In the twenty-first century in which *Falling Man* is set, terrorists are accommodated by, and are positioned against, a global order for which no probable alternative seems available. Terrorism is not about people aiming to change the system anymore, it is "the system itself," to repeat Baudrillard, "which created the objective conditions for this brutal retaliation," for "by seizing all the cards for itself, it forced the Other to change the rules."[45] DeLillo provides a counter-argument against the state's instrumentalisation of trauma through the introduction of Martin's views emphasizing the place U.S. has occupied in world history, a point he draws attention to in his "Ruins" essay:

[T]he primary target of the men who attacked the Pentagon and the World Trade Centre was not the global economy. It was America that drew their fury. It was the high gloss of our modernity. It was the thrust of our technology. It was our perceived godlessness. It was the blunt force of our foreign policy. It was the power of American culture to penetrate every wall, home, life and mind.[46]

The lines DeLillo gives Martin seem to be informed, in part, by Baudrillard's challenging commentary on 9/11. For example, Martin's remarks concerning the goal of the terrorists sound insightful of the paradigmatic shift brought about by globalization: "They strike a blow to this country's dominance. They achieve this, to show how a great power can be vulnerable. A power that interferes, that occupies" (46). And Baudrillard writes:

> The more concentrated the system becomes globally, ultimately forming one single network, the more it becomes vulnerable at a single point. [. . .] Here it was eighteen suicide attackers who, thanks to the absolute weapon of death, enhanced by technological efficiency, unleashed a global catastrophic process.

> When global power monopolizes the situation to this extent, when there is such a formidable condensation of all functions in the technocratic machinery, and when no alternative form of thinking is allowed, what other way is there but a *terroristic situational transfer*? [47]

Similarly, Martin's contention that the twin towers of World Trade Center "were built as fantasies of wealth and power that would one day become fantasies of destruction" (116) invoke Baudrillard's argument that "these architectural monsters [. . .] have always exerted an ambiguous fascination [. . .]—a contradictory feeling of attraction and repulsion, and hence, somewhere, a secret desire to see them disappear."[48] For Baudrillard, the collapse of the towers as a symbolic object—"symbolic of financial power and global economic liberalism"—came about "by a kind of unpredictable complicity—as though the entire system, by its internal fragility, joined in the game of its own liquidation, and hence joined in the game of terrorism."[49]

In his novelization of the event and its impact DeLillo is careful to present different perspectives on 9/11 in juxtaposition, without appearing to be siding with the narratives of either what he defines as state politics or terrorism because "[t]he sense of disarticulation we hear in the term "Us and Them" has never been so striking, at either end."[50] Commenting on the style of the "Ruins" essay, Marco Abel affirms that, "DeLillo's style of response, his aesthetic stance, refuses to hypothesize an essence of 9/11, toward which a subject must subsequently assume a clear position."[51] This equally applies to the writer's fictional encounter with 9/11, which refuses to deliver a definitive account of the event, and instead focuses on the smaller stories "sifted in the ruins of the day." Admittedly, in *Falling Man* his focus falls more on the stories of Americans (and Westerners), in contrast to his portrayal of the terrorists, which has been almost unanimously criticized for being over-simplistic and adding little to the inventory of stereotypes of terrorists. Indeed, not only are the pages allocated to the stories of Americans and the terrorists overtly disproportional, but, apart from the elaborations on Hammad's initial doubts, DeLillo does not attempt at delineating a character available for extensive analysis.

Compared to other post-9/11 works of fiction such as John Updike's *Terrorist* and Mohsin Hamid's *The Reluctant Fundamentalist*, DeLillo's *Falling Man* indeed falls short of accounting for the motivations of the terrorist.[52] Updike's novel, for instance, attempts to investigate the familial and social circumstances in which a half-Irish-American half-Egyptian young man, born and raised in the States, is drawn to terrorism. Updike's Ahmad Ashmawy Mulloy, whose Irish-American mother is portrayed as a morally lax woman and whose Egyptian father has left him when he was still three, seeks to compensate for his disconnectedness in the company of a dubious imam at a small mosque, who, much in the manner of DeLillo's Amir, recruits him for a mission to carry out a suicide bombing. Ahmad's motivation in turning to religion and accepting the suicide mission—which he does not carry out—is his dissatisfaction with the materialism and the lack of moral values in the society in which he lives, "the world, in its American portion, emits a stench of waste and greed, of sensuality and futility."[53] In spite of its shortcomings in representing Islam, Updike's novel, at least, attempts to account for the inner fury of his would-be terrorist with an understanding gaze, whereas DeLillo's terrorists are, in contrast, blinded by an unjustified self-deception: "nobody did any harm to them but they believed Islam was under attack," (83) counterbalanced, partly, by Martin's intellectual analyses. *Terrorist*, is a liberal's questioning of the failures of the multicultural paradise America is considered to be, and of the condition of the marginalized Other, and concludes, unsurprisingly, with a healing closure that projects the familial onto the national. As Rowe writes, "Sentimental in its conclusion [. . .] *Terrorist* nevertheless is a valiant effort by a thoroughly bourgeois writer to employ the techniques of the novel to help American readers comprehend this other-worldly fury."[54] Rowe goes on to argue that "It is not, then, the "failure of the novel as a genre that makes it so difficult for us to "represent" terrorism and terrorists," for, despite its limitations, "the novel can still help us think through an "other," however fraught with problems of language, style, cultural and religious differences, and reader competency this process may be."[55]

Updike's novel fares no better than *Falling Man*, however, in situating terrorism within a global historical context. Mohsin Hamid's novel, *The Reluctant Fundamentalist*, on the other hand, provides an image of America from the perspective of the other, its protagonist Changez, who delivers a first-hand account of the experiences of otherness as opposed to Martin's bookish statements in DeLillo's *Falling Man*. Hamid's narrative of a Princeton-graduate Pakistani young man's transformation into an anti-American activist is bracketed within a frame narrative which is a dinner in Lahore, where Changez and an unnamed American, suggestedly an undercover agent "on a mission" involving Changez, share a meal. Changez, expeditiously articulates his resentment of "the manner in which America [has] conducted itself in the world," through "constant interference in the affairs of the others," including "Vietnam, Korea, the straits of Taiwan, the Middle East, and now Afghanistan" (177). Hamid's novel also points to the systemic anti-Islam hysteria in the aftermath of 9/11, which leads his "reluctant fundamentalist" to his realization that he was "a modern-day janissary, a servant of the American empire at a time when it was invading a country with a kinship to [his]" (173). Although the American appears to be coerced by Changez throughout the encounter to listen to his story, his final gesture of reaching for the gun in his jacket reveals his hostile intent. The parallel Hamid draws between his narrative and *One Thousand and One Arabian Nights* links Changez's position to that of Schederazade, the mythic narrator who must tell the sultan one story after another to forestall her execution. At the novel's ambiguous conclusion the question "Who is the real terrorist?" remains to be answered by the reader who is not given a definitive knowledge of either Changez's links with fundamentalists or the American's identity and motivation.

The reason DeLillo falls short of producing an insightful representation of terrorism and terrorists is, for Rowe, his choice to provide "a searching criticism of our national failings without a complementary understanding of the global forces we have helped to produce and yet have exceeded our cultural, political, and military control."[56] DeLillo's political horizon in *Falling Man* excludes the history of injustice and violence perpetuated by the policies of colonialism, imperialism and neo/colonialism. An old Iraqi man—a baker now living in Hamburg—tells Hammad of his experience during the war between Iran and Iraq. The man, who was then a soldier in Saddam's army in Shatt Al Arab, tells Hammad about the Iranian boys, who were sent to their death—"the martyrs of Ayatollah, here to fall and die" (77)— as part of a military tactic "to divert Iraqi troops and equipment from the real army massing behind front lines" (78). The self-sacrifice of ten thousands of Iranian boys who were "sent out to explode land mines and to run under tanks and into walls of gunfire," made the man think that those boys "were sounding the cry of history, the story of ancient Shia defeat and the allegiance of the living to those who were dead and defeated" (78). DeLillo refrains from acknowledging the role the U.S. has had in the contriving of wars abroad like the one between Iran and Iraq. "Most countries are run by madmen," (78) concludes DeLillo, with his old Iraqi man, in telling disavowal of the historical contexts in which madmen are raised to power. By contrast, Mohsin Hamid's writing in *The Reluctant Fundamentalist* is infused by an historical consciousness that points to the "common strand," in similar conflicts, which his "reluctant fundamentalist" recognizes, a year after the 9/11 attacks, as "the advancement of a small coterie's concept of American interests in the guise of the fight against terrorism, which [is] defined to refer only to the organized and politically motivated killing of civilians by killers *not* wearing the uniforms of soldiers."[57] It is this historical consciousness that informs the accumulated anger of Hamid's Princeton-graduate Pakistani activist who wonders "by what quirk of human history my companions [his American class-mates] were in a position to conduct themselves in the world as though they were its ruling class."[58] The terrorists in *Falling Man* refer to history, too, yet DeLillo denies them the historical insight, which is only partly voiced by Martin, who is not the radical he once was, and who is, not accidentally, a Westerner.

Although *Falling Man*'s thematic concerns arguably lie elsewhere it is hard to disagree with Rowe on DeLillo's reliance on "hypernationalism," Rowe's term for the dominant ideology, "whereby the U.S. state has attempted to incorporate and thereby domesticate global problems."[59] That "one of our greatest critics of the limitations of thinking only from inside the United States,"[60] relies on the U.S. national form in his 9/11 novel, demands considering in relation to literature's function as an ideological apparatus. DeLillo's political horizon in *Falling Man* is indeed limited to a certain perception of democracy inseparable from both the global and class relations it entails. Despite this dominant ideology in which the text seems to be imbued, however, *Falling Man* displays symptoms of unease with its own assumptions in the form of subtle suggestions concerning the global forces the U.S. has helped to produce. The novel does not commit itself to a thorough representation of the terrorists, yet its lengthy elaborations on the thoughts and actions of its other characters do contain instances that are deconstructive of the very discourse that produces divisive categories between terrorists and non-terrorists, and reveal similarities and affinities where absolute difference is presumed.

The stereotypical depiction of the other—the terrorists—in the text seems to embody linguistic and stylistic clues that arguably reflect back a magnified mirror image of the self—the Americans—and are subversive of the binary logic underlying antagonisms. Hammad's hateful perception of Americans, for example, is too banal to be taken seriously: "These people jogging in the park, world domination. These old men who sit in beach chairs, veined white bodies and baseball caps, they control our world" (173). But an equally banal contempt is echoed in Lianne's "They're the ones who think alike, talk alike, eat the same food at the same time.

[. . .] Say the same prayers, word for word, in the same prayer stance, day and night, following the arc of sun and moon" (68). Hammad's doubts about the justifiability of killing innocent people, like Lianne's admission—"She knew this wasn't true" (68)—betray a stifled attempt at relating to the other outside that binary logic. However, on both occasions the outcome of the encounter with the other involves violence as if to attest to the overwhelming power of the discourses surrounding them. The fundamentalist rhetoric instrumental in transforming Hammad into a suicidal murderer finds its counterpart in the anti-terror rhetoric that drives Lianne to assault a neighbor. The passage conveying Lianne's accumulating anger at Elena through indirect speech is repeatedly interrupted by a deadpan narrative voice that points at her exposure to the post-9/11 media bombardment: "She read everything they wrote about the attacks" (67); "She read stories in newspapers until she had to force herself to stop" (67); "She read newspaper profiles of the dead" (68); and finally "Thoughts from nowhere, elsewhere, someone else's" (69). At the end of the passage, however, Lianne goes to sleep "following the arc of sun and moon," as if to point in the direction of a common human condition (70).

In a similar vein, the way poker is treated in the novel provides a good example of how certain traits and patterns of behavior associated with the other as a mark of its inferiority can actually reside in the self. DeLillo devotes four full pages to depict the poker nights Keith used to have with his friends in his apartment where he lived during his eighteen months long separation from his family. A male-only group of six including two lawyers, a bond trader, an adman, a business writer and a mortgage broker gathered weekly on a regular basis at the same place, "rolling their shoulders, hoisting their balls, ready to sit and play, game faced, testing the forces that govern events" (96). The narrator observes the parallels with the business world; for the players these poker games "were the funneled essence, the clear and intimate extract of their daytime initiatives," which required the use of professional skills involving the presumably opposite categories of "intuition and cold-war risk analysis," "cunning and blind luck," as they "waited for the prescient moment" to act (97). The primitive ritualistic aspect is evoked—"they regressed to preliterate folkways, petitioning the dead,"—as well as the presence of potential violence: "There were elements of one's intent to shred the other's gauzy manhood" (97). The games got increasingly more strictly codified, minimizing the dealer's options and maximizing the stakes, "which intensified the ceremony of check-writing for the long night's losers" (97). Other restrictions followed; first food was banned to impose self-discipline and the conditions to be allowed to leave the table were reduced to the "severest bladder-racked urgency or the kind of running bad luck that requires a player to stand at the window looking out on the deep abiding tide of night" (97-8). Then the consumption of alcohol was limited to "darkish liquors [. . .] the manlier tones and deeper and more intense distillations" (98). The imposition of rules were based on the principle "the stupider the better," and were extended to include talks on sports, television, movie titles, and certain words, and "there were always things to ban and rules to make" (99). Although the only version they played was the five-card stud, the name of the game had to be announced each time by the dealer "because where else would they encounter the kind of mellow tradition exemplified by the needless utterance of a few archaic words" (99). A story Martin had once told Keith about four German poker players whose graves were placed to replicate the position they were always seated at the card table for decades, "with two of the gravestones facing the other two, each player in his time-honored place," became a parable for them because it was "a beautiful story about friendship and the transcendent effects of unremarkable habit" (98-9). Although the rules and bans were eventually removed, "they missed, each dealer in turn, calling out the name of one game [. . .] and tried not to wonder what four other players would think of them, in this wallow of wild-man poker, tombstone to tombstone in Cologne" (100).

In spite of the limited space devoted to the sequences from Hammad's life in *Falling Man*, affinities are suggested between the Islamic fundamentalist enemies of the global order and the poker players, who participate, if indirectly, in the perpetuation of that global order by means of their professional activities—at least four of them worked, we infer from the text, at the World Trade Center. The persistent emphasis placed in the text on what poker specifically provides for these men foregrounds male bonding, communal identity, commitment to one single code, self-imposed rules and bans, awe of ritual and myth, intolerance of aberrant thought or behavior and its concomitant aggression. These are concepts and traits which are more readily associated with the fundamentalists, and reinstated through their portrayal in the novel. In Hamburg, the flat on Marienstrasse is frequented by men "becoming total brothers," warranted by their communal identity as "followers of the Prophet" (83). According to their understanding of Islam which is "under attack" (83) from "the West, corrupt of mind and body" (79), the one code they adhere to is provided by the concept of jihad, which they reduce to "the struggle against the enemy, near enemy and far, Jews first, for all things unjust and hateful, and then the Americans" (80). They have their own rituals to perform—the daily prayers—and their own rules to live by—abstinence from sex and over-eating—and self-imposed bans—shaving is not tolerated. Although Hammad may think a trimmed beard would look better "there were rules now, and he was determined to follow them" (83). Critical opinion is not allowed; when he recounts the story of the thousands of Shiite boys who were sacrificed in the name of jihad in a war between two Muslim nations "they stared him down, they talked him down" (80). Aberration is not tolerated either; Hammad is harshly reproached by Amir for "[e]ating all the time, pushing food into [his] face, [being] slow to approach [his] prayers [. . .] [b]eing with a shameless woman, dragging [his] body over hers" (83).

For Keith the poker game "was the one uncomplicated interval of his week, his month [. . .] that was not marked by the blood-guilt tracings of severed connections" (27). The narrator views Keith's pre-9/11 engagement with poker as a "steadfast commitment" (29) made to a group subsequent to the breakdown of his marriage, symmetrical to Lianne's devotion to the story-line sessions she holds with the group of Alzheimer patients. With two out of the novel's six poker players killed in the attacks and one badly injured, the group dissolves and Keith's communication with Terry Cheng, a fellow survivor in the group, does not last long because "poker was the one code they shared and that was over now" (129). Like the terrorists, the poker players create ties through a single code.

Keith's previous engagement with poker becomes, in his post-9/11 existence, an obsessive life-consuming activity which takes him to the gambling parlors of Atlantic City and North-eastern Indian casinos, and finally to Las Vegas where he immerses himself in competitive poker. Poker, it can be argued, provides Keith Neudecker with the means to act out the intense emotions derived from his experience of terror during the attacks, thus overcome his trauma and make a fresh start in life with "a new deck of cards." However, as Kauffman maintains, "Keith is no Gatsby. The fresh green breast of the new world was already receding in the 1920s; the dream of unlimited potential has now disappeared."[61] So, Keith Neudecker's new life—his "new deck" of cards or "new cover"—is one totally engulfed in poker, and he finds himself "fitting into something that was made to his shape" as he is "never more himself than in these rooms, with a dealer crying out a vacancy at table seventeen" (225). The attraction of Vegas for Keith is in the "standard methods and routines" sustained in the artificial environment the city offers. Rather than serving towards the working through of his trauma, poker keeps him in a permanent state of disconnectedness: "These were the times when there was nothing outside, no flash of history or memory that he might unknowingly summon in the routine run of the cards" (225). Poker in *Falling Man* becomes synonymous with terror, which, Charyl Norton remarks, "becomes something so real that it cannot be mediated in language," and Keith has to "find something else to mediate this terror, to vocalize it as he could not, and poker, with its high stakes, isolation and adrenalin, fills that hole."[62] Hence, towards the end of the novel, "three years after the planes" poker supervenes upon all else: "He was looking at five-deuce off-suit. He thought for a moment he might walk out and get the first plane, pack and go [. . .] He folded his cards and sat back. By the time a fresh deck floated up he was ready to play again" (229).

The poker which Keith and his pals played in the past was already described as involving the pleasure of "testing the forces that governed the events." Now it provides Keith with a sense of structure that seems to be missing in his life: "But the game had structure, guiding principles, sweet and easy interludes of dream logic when the player knows that the card he needs is the card that's sure to fall" (211-2). He entertains a sense of control over what appears uncontrollable: "The cards fell randomly, no assignable cause, but he remained the agent of free choice [. . .] in the crucial instant ever repeated hand after hand, the choice of yes or no [. . .] that reminds you who you are. It belonged to him, this yes or no" (211-2). The will to control that Keith finds in the repetitive patterns of the game involves, above all, the intent to master death. The attacks on September 11 have left two of his poker friends dead, another one severely injured. Rumsey, his colleague has died in his arms shortly before he miraculously got out of the burning tower. Now, Keith Neudecker resumes life with a new deck of cards in his hands, and tries to halt death in the closed space of a casino, believing "[t]his was never over. That was the point. There was nothing outside the game but faded space" (189). "With the reckless ferocity of someone who cheated death," Kauffman observes, "Keith devotes himself to tournament gambling."[63] To overcome death one must stop the flow of time, and Keith longs for a moment when temporal indices will become irrelevant. Watching the races at a sports book in Vegas he contemplates: "Races ended, others began, or they were the same races replayed on one or more of the screens. [. . .] He checked his watch again. He knew time and day of week and wondered when such scraps of data would begin to feel disposable" (189). And towards the end of the novel he reaches that point: "He was becoming the air he breathed [. . .] There were no days or times except for the tournament schedule" (230). As Cvek has noted, "Keith's withdrawal into a post-traumatic acting out is thus also significantly marked by a willing loss of memory and historical consciousness."[64]

Keith's post-9/11 life in poker which is marked by anonymity and self-imposed isolation bear traces of his life in the past, only in a more intensified form. If his new vocation in poker turns him into a vagabond travelling from one location to another where international tournaments are held, he has never been a settled person in the first place. When Martin first met him, we are told, he thought of Keith as a displaced person: "This was an American, not a New Yorker, not one of the Manhattan elect," and associates Keith with the pit bull he said he had once owned, "an American breed, developed originally to fight and kill" (44). Feeling displaced and alienated, Keith has eventually drifted away from his role as husband and father and moved out to an apartment in lower Manhattan only because of its proximity to his office. His life between the separation and the attacks is marked by isolation and detachment, except for the weekly poker games with friends. After the attacks his attempt at restoring his marriage and settling into a family life eventually fails. He has had affairs with other women before and his post-9/11 affair with Florence which takes him to her apartment "across from the park" does not lead anywhere either. The idea of becoming like his father does not appeal to him as he finally realizes that he cannot, after all, "become someone of clear and distinct definition, husband and father, finally, occupying a room in three dimensions in the manner of his parents" (157). So, where "nothing else pertain[s]," poker becomes the only thing that has "binding force" (230). As Rowe maintains:

> Even before we witness Keith Neudecker escape the World Trade Center after the 9/11 attacks, we know him to be a "refugee," deeply traumatized and displaced, incapable of dealing with his family life and work, driven relentlessly by forces he does not understand finally to the triviality of competitive poker.[65]

Similarly, Kauffman holds that "Keith's inner migration was well under way long before 9/11; the terrorist attack merely consolidates his previous tendencies toward withdrawal, flight, diversion."[66] His sense of not belonging to any fixed place or identity takes him finally to the gambling parlors where he is drawn to the "crucial anonymity" poker provides in "the mingling of countless lives that had no stories attached" (204). Anonymity is crucial for Hammad, too, for whom "the idea is to go unseen" (172) in Nokomis, Florida, where he is temporarily located for his flight training. Pushing "a cart through the supermarket," the terrorist in disguise, "clean-shaven, in tennis sneakers," (173) "was becoming invisible to these people," as "they were becoming invisible to him" (171). Both men have the detached attitude of the indifferent observer in relation to other people; Keith "[does] not listen to what [is] said around him, the incidental bounce of dialogue, player to player" (227), and knows the name of one poker player only "because it belongs to a dwarf. There is no other reason to know it" (205). Similarly, Hammad "look[s] at women

42

sometimes" like "the girl at the check-out named Meg or Peg" (171). Both of them are equally displaced and have no sense of connection to the places at which they happen to be; Keith "live[s] and work[s] in this room and that" (226-7), riding in taxis "to and from the downtown street where his hotel [is] located" (227). Hammad recalls one man on a visit who "did not know the name of the town they were in" and thinks, "Nokomis. What does it matter?" (174). And for both men the distinction between reality and illusion become indistinct. Conversing with Terry Cheng in a hotel lounge in Vegas, Keith "stared into the waterfall, forty yards away. He realized he didn't know whether it was real or simulated. The flow was unruffled and the sound of falling water might easily be a digital effect like the waterfall itself" (203-4). Similarly for Hammad, "[t]his entire life, this world of lawns to water and hardware stacked on endless shelves, was total, forever, illusion" (173).

Taking up poker as his vocation Keith takes the commitment to the code to its furthest extreme, and what had started as a joke between friends playing poker for leisure becomes the one guiding principle of his life which is ruled by poker, and he cannot help wondering whether he is "becoming a self-operating mechanism, like a humanoid robot that understands two hundred voice commands, far-seeing, touch-sensitive but totally, rigidly controllable" (226). Keith's view of himself at the poker table like "a robot dog with infrared sensors and a pause button, subject to seventy-five voice commands," (226) driven by irresistible external forces is strikingly reminiscent of Hammad in his last minutes in the Hudson corridor, trying to recall the jihadist instructions: "Forget the world. Be unmindful of the thing called the world. [. . .] Recite the sacred words. Pull your clothes tightly about you. Fix your gaze. Carry your soul in your hand" (238). As Rowe convincingly argues:

> In *Falling Man*, Keith Neudecker stumbles blindly out of his office in the World Trade Center back into his dysfunctional family life, an aimless affair with another 9/11 survivor, and then into the bathos of international poker competitions. Initially sympathetic characters, versions of a waning humanism, Gray [in *Mao II*] and Neudecker degenerate into specters of their

terrorist antagonists: aimless, stateless, socially determined
beings following others' orders.[67]

Keith's recklessness and propensity for violence that he shares with
the terrorist is observed by Lianne—"He did not want to be safe"—who
confronts Keith with his desire to kill: "'You want to kill somebody,' she
said. [. . .] 'You've wanted this for some time' she said. [. . .] She
knew there was something that had to be satisfied, a matter discharged
in full, and she thought this was at the heart of his restlessness" (214).
"Too old" to join the army where he "could kill without penalty and then
come home and be a family" (214), Keith's violence is sublimated into the
terror of poker: "Make them bleed. Make them spill their precious losers'
blood" (230). His total surrender to a life in poker reduces his sense of self
to the boundaries set by the game: "The game mattered, the stacking of
chips, the eye count, the play and dance of hand and eye. He was identical
with these with these things" (228). His submissiveness is reminiscent of
Hammad's willful loss of identity, and both men seem to have succumbed
to the idea of predestined end, invalidating the will to meaning: "Most
lives don't make sense" (216) to Keith in the face of the "fact that they
would all be dead one day" (228), as for Hammad "There is no purpose,
this is the purpose" (177).

The theme of death as inevitable end permeates the text and none
of the characters seems to be immune to the anxiety deriving from the
impending doom that awaits them all. As Christine Muller maintains:
"Whether in the form of terminal disease, martyrdom, or surviving
September 11, the specific end concerning each of these characters is
the ultimate end: death."[68] DeLillo's chief device to explore the theme of
disintegration is the Alzheimer motif introduced through Lianne's weekly
storyline sessions with the patients at the early stages of the illness. The
Alzheimer patients in the novel suffer from varying degrees of memory loss
and are doomed to be cut off from their individual histories, evidenced in
their storylines that grow increasingly unintelligible. The disease becomes a
metaphor for the post-9/11 condition which "is progressing exponentially:
history is receding more and more rapidly from us—along with our will,
imagination, and power to anchor it in anything approaching the familiar.

Nor can we fathom what the future holds, except to acknowledge that it will not resemble the past."[69] Obsessed with the memory of her father who had Alzheimer's and chose to kill himself, Lianne worries over her own genetic disposition and projects her own anxiety onto the members of the storyline group. She witnesses her mother's declining health and eventual death. Keith strives to forget his past and loses himself in poker, surrendering fully to life's randomness implicated in the poker game. Similarly, randomness and contingency are what the logic of terrorism is found upon; terror kills randomly and for the terrorist neither the lives of those he kills nor his own have any significance, as long as they "serve the much higher purpose of metaphysical contingency"[70] All of DeLillo's characters, whether believers or not, persistently talk about God, God's will, death and predestination in relation to what happened on September 11, and why. Hence, Florence Givens, the character who seems to have the most genuine faith in God, begins to think that "dying is ordinary," so "why don't we put it in God's hands?" (89-90). Despite being against everything the Americans stand for, the terrorists, too, believe in God, Florence speculates, so perhaps the lesson to be learnt from the experience of 9/11 is to "obey the laws of God's universe, which teach us how small we are and where we're all going to end up" (90). As fate and faith continue to preoccupy the minds of the characters including the terrorists Hammad and Amir, it is the figure of the eponymous performance artist who epitomizes, in his acts of fall, the predestined end awaiting them all: "it could be the name of a trump card in a tarot deck, Falling Man, name in gothic type, the figure twisting down in a stormy night sky" (221). David Janiak, whose name appears in the title of the final part, and who is the eponymous "Falling Man" in the novel in which falling is DeLillo's main trope for designating the process of disintegration manifested in the individual falls experienced by his many characters.

One immediate extra-textual referent for DeLillo's title is Richard Drew's photograph which captured an employee of World Trade Center as he was falling to his death, and appeared briefly in the newspapers on September 12, 2001. The man in the photograph, who was identified as an employee of the Windows on the World Restaurant at World Trade Center was shown falling headfirst, arms at his sides, with one knee bent on a perpendicular line to the column panels of the towers. Although the photograph was rapidly withdrawn due to the heated debates it gave rise to it became a symbol for the people who jumped from the windows of the towers or were blown out by the force of the blast. Tom Junod describes the image of the falling man in the photograph:

> In the picture, he departs from this earth like an arrow. Although he has not chosen his fate, he appears to have, in his last instants of life, embraced it. If he were not falling, he might very well be flying. He appears relaxed, hurtling through the air. He appears comfortable in the grip of unimaginable motion. He does not appear intimidated by gravity's divine suction or by what awaits him. His arms are by his side, only slightly outriggered. His left leg is bent at the knee, almost casually. His white shirt, or jacket, or frock, is billowing free of his black pants. His black high-tops are still on his feet.[71]

Drew's photograph, in which the downward movement of the victim seems frozen in time against the background of the towers is an image of death elevated to the status of aesthetic object in a strictly Aristotelian sense: "There are things which we see with pain so far as they themselves are concerned but whose images, even when executed in very great detail, we view with pleasure."[72] The professional photographer in an earlier DeLillo novel, *Mao II*, has stopped taking pictures of suffering people because of art's inability to show suffering without making it look beautiful: "after years of this I began to think it was somehow, strangely—not valid. No matter what I shot, how much horror, reality, misery, ruined bodies, bloody faces, it was all so fucking pretty in the end."[73] Drew's photograph of the "Falling Man" functions, to a certain extent, in a similar way: it beautifies its object, death, resulting in an aesthetic distance from its factual basis, at the same time as it represents the scare, confusion, and havoc experienced on 9/11. Junod elaborates on the artistic achievement of the photograph:

> The man in the picture [. . .] is perfectly vertical, and so is in accord with the lines of the buildings behind him. He splits them, bisects them: Everything to the left of him in the

picture is the North Tower; everything to the right, the South. Though oblivious to the geometric balance he has achieved, he is the essential element in the creation of a new flag, a banner composed entirely of steel bars shining in the sun.[74]

The emphasis on the aesthetic distance between the represented and its representation which frames and freezes its object spatially and temporally is given extra weight in the novel through repetitive references to still life—natura morta—as an artistic form. In the days following the attacks, one of the Morandi still lifes hanging on the wall of Nina's apartment becomes the subject of a discussion concerning the interpretation of the art object. Nina, who has studied, and written on, Giorgio Morandi's art voices a strictly formalist view of the artistic work—"The work is a fact in itself" (113). The painting in question showing "huddled boxes and biscuit tins, grouped before a darker background," includes "two darks objects," which are "dark and somber, with smoky marks and smudges" (49). In the two tall dark items in the painting that appear to "too obscure to name," Lianne and Martin see "the towers," whereas for Nina "these shapes are not translatable to modern towers, twin towers" (49). Nina insists that the Morandi still life "rejects that kind of extension or projection," and conveys, transhistorically, its inherent meaning which is about "being human, being mortal" (111). For Lianne, on the other hand, in the novel's post-9/11 universe even the Italian term for still life (dead nature) seems "stronger than it had to be, somewhat ominous" (12). The dismal connotations of the term still life can be extended to Drew's photograph showing the falling man frozen in time and space; with its image caught between life and death, the photograph is "the ultimate still life."[75] A representation of the terror of death, however, the photograph, paradoxically conveys feelings of tranquility and surrender: "Despite our knowledge that he is about to die, his tranquility evokes an ascent to Heaven whilst his downward trajectory mimics the descent to Hell."[76] In the novel, the same photograph effects a similar reaction in Lianne: Headlong, freefall, she thought, and this picture burned a hole in her mind and heart, dear God, he was a falling angel and his beauty was horrific" (222).

However, the referent for the titular falling man of DeLillo's novel turns out to be not the iconic image in Richard Drew's photograph, but the performance artist named David Janiak, publicly known as "Falling Man", who begins to appear in the streets of post-9/11 New York with his performances in which he re-enacts the fall from the tower, jumping from bridges, elevated railway tracks and other high edifices. His performances always come unannounced, and he does not allow his falls to be recorded or televised, therefore the audience is limited to the number of people who happen to be on location at the time of the event. In the novel, the link between his performed falls and the image in Drew's photograph remains obscure: "[t]here is some dispute over the issue of the position he assumed during the fall, the position he maintained in his suspended state," and "if this photograph was an element in his performances he said nothing about it when questioned by reporters after one of his arrests" (221-2). Like the man in Drew's photograph whose downward movement seems frozen in space and time, Janiak's performed falls with one leg attached to the end of a barely visible string that keeps him floating in midair freeze the action, if only temporarily. With his pose evoking that of the man in Drew's photograph, DeLillo's fictional Janiak seems to provide, in the traditional sense, a representation of a representation, which is twice removed from the reality to which it refers—that of the actual man falling to his death. Interestingly, it is again through Lianne's eyes that we witness Janiak's performance which is arguably the theatrical rendering of still life, his dangling figure suspended in midair a reminder of the fatal end that befell the actual victim(s): "A man was dangling there, above the street, upside down. He wore a business suit, one leg bent up, arms at his sides. A safety harness was barely visible, emerging from his trousers at the straightened leg and fastened to the decorative rail of the viaduct" (33). Differently from her response to the photograph, however, Lianne is disturbed by the sight of Janiak dangling from the steel structure outside Grand Central Station, "the single falling figure that trails a collective dread, body come down among us all," and thinks, "this little theatre piece, disturbing enough to stop traffic and send her back into the terminal" (33).

Lianne's first sighting of Falling Man comes ten days after the attacks and her terror is shared by the other viewers who "[shout] up at him, outraged at the spectacle, the puppetry of human desperation" (33). Her second encounter with the performance artist takes place thirty-six days after the attacks, on her way back from a meeting with the Alzheimer patients in Harlem, and this time she watches Janiak making his preparations for the performance. The man appears in the elevated track area, moves to the maintenance platform over the street, affixes the safety harness to the rail of the platform, then stands poised on the rail as people in the windows and on the street wait for his fall. Lianne realizes that Janiak is "waiting for a train to come," because he wants "an audience in motion, passing scant yards from his standing figure" (164). His intention, Lianne speculates, is to re-create the exact same terror experienced by the witnesses who have seen the actual victims falling from the towers on September 11. Some of the commuters on the train would "see him standing," and some would "see him jump," and they would all be "jarred out of their reveries or their newspapers or muttering stunned into their cell phones" (165). Incognizant of the safety harness, "they would only see him fall out of sight," and grope for their cell phones to "describe what they've seen or what others nearby have seen and are now trying to describe to them" (165). Lianne is terrorized but there is something compelling in Janiak's act which holds her spellbound as she watches: "But why was she standing here watching? Because she saw her husband somewhere near. She saw his friend, the one she'd met, or the other, maybe, or made him up and saw him, in a high window with smoke flowing out" (167). The immediacy of the act and its impact as lived experience is conveyed by the shift in the narration to the present tense: "The train comes slamming through and he turns his head and looks into it (into his death by fire) and then brings his head back around and jumps. Jumps or falls. He keels forward, body rigid, and falls full-length, headfirst" (167-8). There is "something awful about the stylized pose, body and limbs, his signature stroke," but "the worst of it" is "the stillness itself and her nearness to the man" (168).

Although Lianne remains disturbed by the performance and the final pose of the dangling man recoiled above the pavement, she finds an explanation for her compulsion to watch when she notices another spectator, "the derelict, the old, threadbare man," equally entranced by the extraordinary spectacle he is witnessing, "seeing something elaborately different from what he encountered step by step in the ordinary run of hours" (168). The revival of the act of falling provides the viewer, Lianne acknowledges, with the means "to learn how to see it correctly, find a crack in the world where it might fit" (168). Watching the derelict watching Janiak's performance, Lianne articulates the irresistible impulse to come to terms with the events that took place on September 11, through an aesthetic experience. As Duvall remarks,

> Motion, then, is something that DeLillo's *Falling Man* restores to the aesthetic meditation on 9/11. Janiak's art combines the chilling sense of falling, a continuity that cannot be perceived as a discrete series of sequenced moments, with the power of Drew's photograph to arrest that same motion. In the disturbing, transgressive art that DeLillo's performance artist Falling Man produces, an art that invokes (and perhaps transcends) Drew's forbidden image of 9/11, the possibility for a degree of healing arises.[77]

When, after Janiak's death, Lianne remembers her reaction to the performance, she intuitively interprets Janiak's art in a way which opposes her mother's conventional view of the work of art, possessing an inherent meaning to be discovered by the viewer: "There were no photographs of that fall. She was the photograph, the photosensitive surface. That nameless body coming down, this was hers to record and absorb" (223). Nor is the artist's intended meaning relevant to subjective interpretation. As Jenkins reminds, "the meaning of an act does not reside solely within the intentionality of the actor, indeed, in most instances it resides within the context of the act's reception. Phenomenological insights or the bedrock of what we now call social constructionism advise us that meaning is located within social situations."[78] However, although the experience of 9/11 provides the context from which the meaning of the performance can be generated, individual perceptions are bound to vary depending on the specific identity, position and history of the individual. In Lianne's case, Janiak's fall is associated with her husband's life in suspense, and his friend Rumsey's actual death during the attack as well as with the members of the Alzheimer group in perpetual decline and her father who "died by his own hand" (169). As Duvall argues, "the individual (such as Lianne) who encounters the work of art is still an individual, not a collectivity. As such, the individual is not solely constituted by some collective trauma but is already the bearer of previous private traumas."[79]

At some level, it is tempting to view Janiak as a surrogate for DeLillo himself, both artists attempting to elicit an aesthetic response to an irreducible event which has already been appropriated through its endless media reproduction. For Andrew O'Hagan both are failed attempts because the performance artist in *Falling Man* "can do no better than constitute some figurative account of the author himself."[80] Thus, Janiak's mid-air suspensions that fail to exactly replicate the freefall of the actual victims ending on the ground are a metaphor for the author's "failure [. . .] to imagine September 11."[81] Brauner, on the other hand, draws attention to the "undeniably powerful"[82] effect of Janiak's performances, and suggests that DeLillo might benefit from the analogy as his novel "both directly confronts and subtly averts its gaze from, the horrors of 9/11, providing its readers with a double vision of events that paradoxically articulates their ineffability."[83]

There is more, however, to the admittedly credible analogy between author and artist in DeLillo's novel than the somewhat simplistic account of the writer creating a surrogate figure to metaphorically and metafictionally stand for his attempts to imagine and articulate the horrors of the event which is 9/11. For one thing, the equation between the writer and his fictional construction of the artist cannot be adequately discussed without taking into account the inherently transgressive nature of performance art, in particular the transgressive gist of David Janiak's falls. In its refusal of the Aristotelian conception of art as removed from reality, and of conventional theatre's reliance on the distance between stage and audience, performance art claims to not imitate but communicate the real as bodily experience, thus violate the distance between art and life. In line with performance art's distrust of language and its representational claim, Janiak's falls—performances without a text—as well his persistent refusal to comment on his art—"He had no comments to make to the media on any subject" (222)—accentuate his rejection of language in favor of an absolute emphasis on the material presence of the body. Janiak's performance obliterates the distinction between the real and the fictional by thrusting the actual body into the space where the viewed and the viewer become accomplices in providing the context from which the meaning of the performance generates.

Secondly, it is through the unmediated materiality of the body that Janiak's act induces an overwhelming feeling of fear and anxiety which is similar to the impact of the terrorist act. As Cvek observes, "Janiak's art is completely in line with the logic of terrorism," as both the terrorist and the performance artist offer "the pure body, without any words of explanation": "This desire for immediacy is what connects Janiak's controversial acts with the violence of the terrorists—both are tactics against what the novel constructs as the repressive surveillance technologies of the state."[84] In addition, the spectacular component in a terrorist act as vast in scale as 9/11 should be considered in terms of its approximation of performance art. In their discussion of the transgressive nature of the suicide attacks on World Trade Center, Frank Lentricchia and Jodie McAuliffe, in *Crimes of Art and Terror*, compare the terrorists' act to performance art:

> In spite of their intentions [. . .] the suicide terrorists who struck New York may be said to have made—with the cooperation of American television—performance art with political designs on its American audience. The site, the World Trade Center, was unconventional and politically loaded: the symbolic center of globalized capitalism. Advanced technology was mastered and put into play. The cast was huge; bodies were subjected to serious pain. All of this in real time, with no element of pretense or make-believe in it. Thanks to the cameras, which bin Laden could confidently assume would be there, images of a spectacular sort were generated, framed, and replayed endlessly. Thanks to the presence of the camera, which guaranteed a vast audience, this act of performance means something, achieves the paradoxical fusion of "life" and "art," "event" and its filmic representation in minute and faithful reproduction.[85]

This constitutes "part of the problem facing DeLillo in addressing 9/11": "the terrorist has usurped the role of politicizing the image. If the avant-garde modernist hoped to shock the bourgeoisie, that is precisely the role that the terrorist plays in contemporary society."[86] DeLillo attempts to counter both the terrorist's usurpation of the image to create shock, and the state's politicization of the image to turn trauma into an instrument to justify hegemonic wars disguised as retaliatory action through his depiction of the performance artist known as Falling Man. DeLillo's performance artist is "particularly tantalizing because he purposely avoids the celebrity that most of the culture craves."[87] Janiak insists on remaining a marginal artist; he does not want publicity and does not allow his art to be assimilated into the media-driven culture in which visual technologies function as the apparatus of state control, and "politics are reduced to images."[88] As opposed to the function of the media as an ideological state apparatus which, by reducing politics to aesthetics, manufactures public consent for its "Us against Them" rhetoric, the image is politicized through the agency of the fictional performance artist. Lentricchia and McAuliffe end their book by an imaginary dialog between Mohammad Atta and Heinrich von Kleist. The pairing of the suicide-terrorist and the suicide-writer, whose act of murder-suicide the authors call the first performance art lends further emphasis to their assertion that "[t]he impulse to create transgressive art and the impulse to commit violence lie perilously close to each other."[89] DeLillo's performance artist does not commit suicide as his ascendant Kleist did, nevertheless the element of suicide is entailed in his self-destructive act—his eventual death is related to injuries caused by his falls—not to mention his posthumously disclosed plans for a suicidal fall with no harness. Arguably then, there is a sense in which Janiak's falling performance can be said to relate to the events on 9/11 in its evoking of the suicidal act of the novel's terrorist, Hammad, who is among the many falling men of the novel in which the parallels between the artist's performance and that of the suicide terrorist are implicitly suggested. Interestingly, whereas the terrorist is given a name and a voice in the narrative, Janiak remains, in the fashion of a real terrorist, anonymous and discreet throughout, and his identity is disclosed only posthumously: "A man named David Janiak, 39 [. . .] the performance artist known as Falling Man"(219).

The terrorist's act is murderous but at the same suicidal; Janiak subjects his body to risk and serious pain, "[h]is falls were said to be painful and highly dangerous due to the rudimentary equipment he used," (222) and his eventual death is linked to his performed falls. Before his somehow mysterious death "apparently of natural causes," (220) probably related to his "chronic depression due to a spinal condition," (222) Janiak is said to have been planning a final suicidal fall with no safety measures. The suicidal element in his work is underscored as Lianne reads in his obituary about his planned final performance: "Plans for his final jump at some unforeseen future did not include a harness, according to his brother Roman Janiak, 44, who spoke to a reporter shortly after he identified the body" (223). Unlike the victim(s) whose fall from the towers can hardly be considered a choice, Janiak's performance is, like the terrorist's, an act of free will characterized by deliberate purpose, training and planning and intended to create a shocking impact on its audience. To borrow from Duvall, "[w]ith the trauma of 9/11 so fresh, Falling Man's art is an outrage. One might say that Falling Man is a terrorist of perception."[90] His conflation of art and reality is, for Lianne, "too near and deep, too personal" (33) not to arouse terror. Like the terrorist who strikes unexpectedly, Janiak whose preparations are equally clandestine—and meticulous—appears unannounced. As Jen Bartlett maintains:

> Janiak's terror-inducing actions in creating an artistic spectacle are the first of DeLillo's methods exploring the theory that terror through spectacle is art. His sudden unexpected appearances echo the 9/11 attacks. There is a certain background level of suspicion attached to him; he is known to operate in New York and the content of his performances are predictable. This dossier of information notwithstanding, the physical and temporal locations of his appearances are as unknown, and consequently as traumatic, as the activities of a well-known terrorist such as Osama Bin Laden. It is not a question of 'if' he will appear, or attack in the case of Bin Laden; it is a case of 'when'. The Falling Man possesses the element of shock and thus is similarly in possession of great power. DeLillo appears to support the concept that the artist is a transgressive figure.[91]

Similar to his treatment of terrorists in the earlier novels from *Libra* to *Mao II*, DeLillo, in *Falling Man*, both "admires and detests their destructive powers, just as he is enchanted and disgusted by their perverse cosmopolitanism."[92] All of DeLillo's terrorists including Kennedy's assassin Oswald in *Libra*, the Lebanese kidnappers in *Mao II*, and the suicide hijackers in *Falling Man* "change the world through destruction, and for that very reason they are compared often and agonizingly to the novelist, either DeLillo or his surrogate, like Bill Gray in *Mao II*."[93] In *Mao II*, in which it has been argued that "DeLillo had already written his great 9/11 novel, long before the specific date and the event happened to come around,"[94] DeLillo had already voiced this subversive view of the novelist's art:

> There is a curious knot that binds novelists and terrorists. In the West we become famous effigies as our books lose the power to shape and influence. [. . .] Years ago I used to think it was possible for a novelist to alter the inner life of the culture. Now bomb-maker and gunmen have taken that territory. They make raids on human consciousness. What writers used to do before we were all incorporated.[95]

Put into the mouth of DeLillo's stand-in character, the novelist Bill Gray, these remarks come out as part of a discussion comparing the role of the novelist to that of the terrorist. In *Mao II* the terrorist seems to have the upper hand as terrorism becomes the narrative of our age while the writer's role "to alter the inner life of the culture," by making "raids on human consciousness," becomes less and less significant in a world in which the narrative of terrorism has replaced the novel in shaping social consciousness: "Beckett is the last writer to shape the way we think and see. After him, the major work involves midair explosions and crumbled buildings. This is the new tragic narrative."[96]

In support of the argument positioning the artist and the terrorist on a par in terms of their acts of transgression, the appearance of the name David Janiak as the title of the novel's final part becomes all the more significant put in juxtaposition with the two other terror-associated names figuring as the titles of the first and second parts: Bill Lawton and Ernst Hechinger. DeLillo's spotlighting of those three names in his titles is suggestive of the transgressive links he establishes between the terrorist and the artist. The positioning of the part "Ernst Hechinger" in the middle—an ex-terrorist turned art dealer, although he is presently neither a terrorist nor an artist—makes Martin a mediator between the parts "Bill Lawton" and "David Janiak", suggesting that "art might still vie with terrorism in shaping American imagination."[97] By extension then, if the artist is, as has been argued, a metaphor for the writer then DeLillo can be said to insinuate a comparison between the terrorist and the novelist—the theme he has more elaborately explored in *Mao II*.

Through the literary representation of a performance artist, DeLillo produces a narrative around the figure of "Falling Man" whose art resists the logic of representation and, as Francesco Pontuale maintains, "is meant to retrieve an irreducible event that because of its endless media reproduction is destined to be forgotten, if not removed altogether."[98] Thus, the insertion of the artist-terrorist David Janiak into his novel can be said to constitute DeLillo's own act of transgression through his personal art of writing. By describing Janiak's act from the perspective of Lianne, DeLillo refuses to provide an authorial comment on the meaning of his performance and instead conveys its impact on the viewer. As opposed to the tranquilizing effect of the photographic image of the falling man on Lianne, David Janiak's act in *Falling Man* not only re-enacts the trauma itself as a bodily lived experience, but also its impact on his viewers simulates the original moment as the news of his performances is spread through his witnesses "by cell phone, intimately, as in the towers and in the hijacked planes" (165). Janiak's art constitutes what Leonard Wilcox calls an "aesthetic of resistance"[99] to a regime of media and spectacle, and its unmediated violent foray into the viewer's consciousness constitutes a counter-hegemonic practice.

DeLillo, in his turn, attempts to resist the state's instrumentalisation of trauma through representation, and instead of trying to represent 9/11, offers the reader a confrontation with the thing itself. However, the re-presentation of "the thing" in the text remains contained by the political vision that avoids the discussion of the historical. The performance of the novel's artist "as a Brechtian dwarf," (223) whose training has included "formal classes six days a week in both Cambridge and Moscow," (222) involves the Brechtian device of defamiliarization. However his presentation in the text is not accompanied by the element of historicization which, Brecht insists, is what defamiliarization is about. Thus, the text's transgression becomes an aborted attempt in its refusal to provide commentary on the historicity of the moment it so vividly describes without contextualizing it in world history. Therefore, even if *Falling Man* can be considered an attempt at the counternarrative DeLillo has said he needed as an internal counterweight to the manipulative inscriptions of 9/11, it is also a meta-fictional meditation on the limitations of his art. The concluding image of the novel is not his fictional construct of the transgressive artist but a shirt falling from the towers. As the narrative returns to the discursive "now" of 9/11 the shirt Keith sees "[coming] down out of the high smoke, [. . .] lifted and drifting in the scant light and then falling again, down toward the river," (4) re-emerges: "Then he saw a shirt come down out of the sky. He walked and saw it fall, arms waving like nothing in this life" (246). The novel's recounting of the series of falls instigated by the collapse of the towers ends with the image of a shirt, literally disembodied, and unidentifiable. Considering the temporal structure of the narrative forestalling the possibility of moving on, the return of the shirt seems to point to a defeat for the artist whose transgressive acts involve the desire "to put a body back in that white shirt."[100] Janiak dies three years after the attacks; his death taking place in the discursive "after" of the novel—but the "now" of the narrative—reinforces the pessimism concerning the future. DeLillo's *Falling Man*, like Janiak's art, performs the original trauma in the form of a counter-hegemonic practice to the state's instrumentalisation of the trauma, yet its transgressive gesture closes upon itself and remains indefinitely suspended in a permanent now.

NOTES to PART I

1 Don DeLillo, *Falling Man* (Picador, London, 2011). All subsequent references will be made to that edition.

2 Sven Cvek, "Killing Politics: The Art of Recovery in Falling Man," 335.

3 Cvek, 335.

4 Christoph Amend and Georg Diez, "I Don't Know America Anymore". [This interview originally appeared in *Die Zeit* magazine on 11 October 2007.] http://dumpendebat.net/static-content/delillo-diezeit-Oct2007.html.   Web. 24 April 2011.

5 Don DeLillo, "In the Ruins of the Future: Reflections on Terror and Loss in the Shadow of September," *Harpers Magazine*, December 2001, 38.

6 The civil rights attorney alluded to in the novel is Lynne Stewart who was found guilty in 2005 of distributing press releases on behalf of her jailed client Sheikh Omar Abdel-Rahman,—the Blind Sheikh—the Egyptian cleric convicted of planning terrorist attacks. Stewart, accused of aiding the cause of terrorism, was initially sentenced to 28 months of prison time, and was re-sentenced in 2010 to ten years in prison in light of her alleged perjury at her trial and her lack of remorse after her initial sentencing.

7 Linda S. Kauffman, "Bodies in Rest and Motion in *Falling Man*," in Olster, 141.

8 Don DeLillo, "In the Ruins", 39.

9 DeLillo, "In the Ruins", 35.

10 DeLillo, "In the Ruins", 34.

11 DeLillo, "In the Ruins", 34.

12 Linda S. Kauffman, "The Wake of Terror: Don Delillo's 'In The Ruins of The Future,' 'Baader-Meinhof,' and *Falling Man*," 356.

13 Amend and Diez.

14 Cvek, 333.

15 David Brauner, "'The Days After' and 'The Ordinary Run of Hours': Counternarratives and Double Vision in Don DeLillo's *Falling Man*," 76.

16 Cvek, 332-33.

17 John N. Duvall, "Witnessing Trauma: *Falling Man* and Performance Art," in Olster, 152.

18 Cvek, 331.

19 Kauffmann, "Bodies in Rest," 150.

[20] Amend and Diez.

[21] Kauffman, "Bodies in Rest," 139.

[22] John Carlos Rowe, "Global Horizons in *Falling Man*," in Olster, 126.

[23] Rowe, 125.

[24] Rowe, 125-6.

[25] Rowe, 126.

[26] Kauffman, "The Wake of Terror," 369.

[27] Cvek, 333.

[28] DeLillo, "In the Ruins," 33.

[29] DeLillo, "In the Ruins," 39.

[30] Rowe, 123-4.

[31] DeLillo, "In the Ruins," 33.

[32] Another allusion to domestic terrorists in the novel is made through the "Unaflyer," a retired aeronautical engineer who has written a book which "seems to predict what happened," as it "contains a long sort of treatise on plane hijacking [...] many documents concerning the vulnerability of certain airports," and "names many things that actually happened or happening now," such as "Wall Street, Afghanistan"(138-9). The nickname for the writer recalls Ted Kaczinsky, the Unabomber, who, from 1978 to 1995 sent 16 mail bombs to targets in the U.S.A., killing 3 people and injuring 23, and wrote a manifesto indicting scientists for their complicity in the erosion of human freedom by modern technologies.

[33] Kauffman, "The Wake of Terror," 362.

[34] Jean Baudrillard, "The Violence of the Global," in Baudrillard, 87.

[35] Baudrillard, "The Violence," 90.

[36] Baudrillard, "The Violence," 91-2.

[37] Baudrillard, "The Violence," 92-3.

[38] The information Rowe provides on Kommune One is as follows:
Kommune 1, or "K1," was a short-lived political commune founded in Berlin in 1967 by a group of radicals led by Dieter Kunzelmann, Rudi Dutschke, Bernd Rabehl, and including Hans Magnus Enzensberger's ex-wife, Dagrun, and his brother, Ulrich. By 1969, this anti-government student activist group had fallen apart, but in its heyday was known for planning and occasionally carrying out Dadaist-style "performance" acts of social satire. Such acts included the planned "Pudding Assassination" of Vice President Hubert Humphrey during his visit to Berlin in April 1967—so called because one

plan called for attacking him with pudding, yogurt, and flour—and the famous K1 photograph of communards' buttocks posed against a wall with the headline: *"Das Private ist politisch!"* ("The personal is political!"). The symbolic actions of Kommune 1 were usually linked to specific political acts, such as their demonstration against the Shah of Iran's visit to Berlin on 2 June 1967, but they were often criticized by German left-activists as more interested in publicity than in political change. (Rowe, 127)

[39] DeLillo, "In the Ruins," 40.

[40] In *Mao II*, too, DeLillo's characters talk about the towers. Brita, the photographer complains that "everything human about the lower island [is] being hauled away so they can build their towers" (39).

[41] DeLillo, "In the Ruins," 33.

[42] DeLillo, "In the Ruins," 40.

[43] DeLillo, "In the Ruins," 38.

[44] Don DeLillo, *Mao II* (Vintage, London, 1992).

[45] Jean Baudrillard, "The Spirit of Terrorism," in Baudrillard, 9.

[46] DeLillo, "In the Ruins," 33.

[47] Baudrillard, "The Spirit," 8-9.

[48] Jean Baudrillard, "Requiem for the Twin Towers," in Baudrillard, 41-2.

[49] Baudrillard, "Requiem," 43-45.

[50] DeLillo, "In the Ruins," 34.

[51] Marco Abel, *Violent Affect: Literature, Cinema, and Critique After Representation* (University of Nebraska Press, Lincoln, 2008), 217.

[52] John Updike, *Terrorist* (Knopf, New York, 2006) and Mohsin Hamid, *The Reluctant Fundamentalist* (Harcourt Books, Florida, 2007).

[53] Updike, 109.

[54] Rowe, 133.

[55] Rowe, 133-4.

[56] Rowe, 134.

[57] Mohsin Hamid, 202.

[58] Mohsin Hamid, 24.

[59] Rowe, 134.

[60] Rowe, 134.

[61] Kauffman, "The Wake of Terror," 368.

[62] Charly Norton, "Terror as Text: Delillo's *Falling Man* and The Representation of Poker as Terror," in Vardalos, 181.

[63] Kauffman, "The Wake of Terror," 369.

[64] Cvek, 333.

[65] Rowe, 124.

[66] Kauffman, "Bodies in Rest," 147.

[67] Rowe, 122.

[68] Christin Muller, "Fate and Terror in Don Delillo's Falling Man," in Vardalos, 167.

[69] Kauffman, "The Wake of Terror," 368.

[70] Rowe, 123.

[71] Tom Junod, "The Falling Man," www.esquire.com.8September2009. Web. 5 January 2010. [The article first appeared on *Esquire*, September 2003.]

[72] Aristotle, *Poetics* (The University of Michigan Press, the U.S.A, 1994), 20.

[73] Don DeLillo, *Mao II*, 24-5.

[74] Junod.

[75] Jen Bartlett, "Cultivated Tragedy: Art, Aesthetics, and Terrorism in Don Delillo's Falling Man", 7. http://startrek.ccs.yorku.ca/~topia/docs/turningon/Bartlett.pdf. Web. 7 May 2011.

[76] Bartlett, 6-7.

[77] Duvall, "Witnessing Trauma," 167.

[78] Chris Jenks, *Transgression* (Routledge, London and New York, 2003), 8.

[79] Duvall, "Witnessing Trauma," 167.

[80] Andrew O'Hagan, "Racing Against Reality," *The New York Review of Books*, 28 June 2007. http://www.nybooks.com/articles/archives/2007/jun/28/racing-against-reality/. Web. 11 October 2010.

[81] O'Hagan.

[82] Brauner, 74.

[83] Brauner, 81.

[84] Cvek, 347-8.

[85] Frank Lentricchia and Jody McAuliffe, *Crimes of Art and Terror* (The University of Chicago Press, Chicago, 2003), 13-42.

[86] Duvall, "Witnessing Trauma," 155.

[87] Kauffmann, "Bodies in Rest," 148.

[88] Duvall, "Witnessing Trauma," 153.

[89] Lentricchia and McAuliffe, "An Interview with Frank Lentricchia and Jodie McAuliffe," http://www.press.uchicago.edu/Misc/Chicago/472051in.html Web. 9 July 2011.

[90] Duvall, "Witnessing Trauma," 159.

[91] Bartlett, 5.

[92] Rowe, 122.

[93] Rowe, 121.

[94] Tobby Litt, "The Trembling Air (Review of *Falling Man*)," *The Guardian*, 26 May 2007. http://www.guardian.co.uk/books/2007/may/26/fiction.dondelillo. Web. 18 November 2010.

[95] DeLillo, Mao II, 41.

[96] DeLillo, *Mao II*, 157.

[97] Duvall, "Witnessing Trauma," 156.

[98] Francesco Pontuale, "Some Stories Never End: DeLillo and Foer's Falling Men," Proceedings of the 20th AISNA Conference (Torino, 24-26 September 2009), 4.

[99] Leonard Wilcox, "Terrorism and Art: Don DeLillo's *Mao II* and Jean Baudrillard's *The Spirit of Terrorism*," *Mosaic* (39; 2, June 2006), 102.

[100] Kauffman, "Bodies in Rest," 135.

PART II

. . . .

"DARKNESS IMPLACABLE": CORMAC

MCCARTHY'S *THE ROAD*

There is no document of civilization which is not at the same time a document of barbarism.
—Benjamin, *Illuminations*

DeLillo's *Falling Man* ends in the discursive now of 9/11. Its entropic mood precluding the possibility of imagining the future is encapsulated in Lianne's statement that "Nothing is next. There is no next" (10). The same precept governs Cormac McCarthy's *The Road*: "There is no later. This is later" (56).[1] McCarthy's tenth novel which appeared in 2006, a year before DeLillo's novel, is a meditation on that unimaginable future, expanding on the mood of entropy that permeates *Falling Man*. *The Road* envisions a "next" protruded into an apocalyptic future shorn of historical markers except for an unidentified catastrophe that has brought the world to the brink of utter annihilation. Essentially a journey narrative recounting the story of a father and son traveling through a postapocalpytic landscape in an attempt to survive, the novel draws from the genres of apocalyptic and dystopian fiction, gothic literature and traditional lament narratives. The image of the waste land provides an intertextual link to T.S. Eliot's poem *The Wasteland* while evoking the pilgrims' stories set in desolate landscapes through its biblical allusions and resonances. Time and place in this apparently biblical allegory are left unidentified although the topographic markers set it readily within the southeastern United States, and there is ample textual evidence to qualify the novel as a specifically American nightmare.

The plot of the novel comprises a linear survival story, told by a third person narrator. In the aftermath of an unspecified catastrophe that has happened roughly ten years ago, and has turned the natural landscape into a desolate wasteland, a man and his son are on a southward journey to the ocean in the hope of finding a place which might provide them with relatively better climactic conditions for survival. The man's wife, we are told, has chosen suicide at some point along the journey, leaving behind her husband and her son to whom she has given birth shortly after the catastrophe. The father and son keep walking day after day, dragging along a shopping cart for storing their scarce belongings, and armed with nothing but a pistol with two bullets, a map, and a pair of binoculars to help them in their struggle for survival. The man seems to have an unshakable faith that they are the "good guys carrying the fire," and that his son is implicated in a divine scheme concerning the fate of humanity that has been apparently reduced to a level of bare animalistic behavior—including cannibalism—aimed no more than at mere survival. The plot flows with the detailed accounts of the endeavors of the two protagonists, ill-equipped to protect themselves from the incredibly harsh climactic conditions, feeding on whatever comes across as edible, fighting against exhaustion and illness, and trying to hide from the cannibalistic tribes, and hordes of thieves and scavengers. The man, self-justified in his south-bound divine mission, is ardently committed to do whatever it takes to accomplish it: he shoots to death a man who threatens to kill his son, wounds another, forces a thief to take off all his clothes, practically sending him to his death, refuses to care for other human beings, and only helps one old man with some food when his son insists. They finally reach their destination, the south which hardly offers any better prospects for survival, and the man, worn out by the disease he has suffered from throughout the journey, dies. The boy is discovered by a man, who assures him that he means no harm, and helps him cover his father's dead body in a blanket. After inquiring about the people the man lives with, the boy accepts his offer to go with him. The plot ends with the image of the boy in the care of a pious and caring woman in whom he seems to have found a surrogate mother.

Critics have been quick to position the novel within the context of the global political climate in the aftermath of the 9/11 attacks, and as Tim Edwards notes, "a storyline that just a few short years ago would have seemed more naturally suited to the Cold War era has taken on a greater urgency in a post-9/11 world."[2] John Cant argues that Cormac McCarthy's tenth novel *The Road* is "a retrospective on the author's own previous works," preoccupied with "The grand Narrative of Western culture," with particular focus on its "variant known as American Exceptionalism," and always presenting it "within its broader cultural context, and also identifying it as a product of changing historical circumstances."[3] Cant goes on to observe that the novel's "apocalyptic tone reflects the mood of America following the destruction of the World Trade Centre (if not its religiosity), just as [. . .] *Blood Meridian* reflected the mood generated by the Vietnam War."[4] Alan Warner, too, sees McCarthy's other nine novels as "rungs" leading to *The Road* "as a pinnacle," that "needs a context in both the past and in so-called post-9/11 America."[5] For Chris Walsh, "the dystopian view [*The Road*] offers is very much in keeping with the ideological eye-glass, so to speak, of its time of composition and publication."[6] Walsh links the novel's post-apocalyptic vision to "the dystopian sensibility which has informed the nation's imaginative consciousness in the aftermath of September 11, the sorry mess of a war in Iraq which constitutes a grim episode in the history of American exceptionalism," as well as "the specter of global warming and ecological disaster, and the implications of economic globalization and trans-nationalism."[7] Cant, similarly, draws attention to the "extreme images," in the novel which are "drawn from everyday reality that were apocalyptic indeed," and which are "conjured by very real fears concerning global warming and climate change," as well as "the war in Iraq," and "the horrors associated with Abu Ghraib and Guantanamo Bay."[8] Alan Warner maintains that "this text, in its fragility, exists uneasily within such ill times," and worries that "its nightmare vistas [could] reinforce those in the US who are determined to manipulate its people into believing that terror came into being only in 2001": "It's perverse that the scorched earth which *The Road* depicts often brings to mind those real apocalypses of Southern Iraq beneath black oil smoke, or New Orleans—vistas not unconnected with the contemporary American regime."[9]

The stylistic characteristics of *The Road* reflect on a world which has been made "a lie every word" (79). The visual intensity of a wasted world is expressed in the descriptions of landscape infused with images of death and decay:

> Charred and limbless trunks of trees stretching away on every side. Ash moving over the road and the sagging hands of blind wire strung from the blackened lightpoles whining thinly in the wind. A burned house in a clearing and beyond that a reach of meadowlands stark and gray and a raw red mudbank where a roadworks lay abandoned. Farther along were bill boards advertising motels. Everything as it once had been save faded and weathered. (6)

Frozen in an apparently everlasting present, the shattered world of the novel translates into a syntactic pattern in which main verbs and temporal indices are usually absent in landscape descriptions. Likewise, the descriptions of deserted towns abundant with nouns but devoid of verbs imprint the images of waste and ruin with an effect equivalent to photographic accuracy:

> Tall clapboard houses. Machinerolled metal roofs. A log barn in a field with an advertisement in faded ten-foot letter across the roofslope. See Rock City. [. . .] A television set. Cheap stuffed furniture together with an old handmade cherrywood chifforobe. [. . .] A child's room with a stuffed dog on the windowsill looking out at the garden. (20-21)

Travelling through "[b]urnt forests for miles along the slopes and snow," the man and the boy can see "[n]o tracks in the road, nothing living anywhere" (30). In the cities where there was once life they come across the "mummied dead everywhere": "The flesh cloven along the bones, the ligaments dried to tug and taut as wires. Shriveled and drawn like latterday bogfolk, their faces of boiled sheeting, the yellowed palings of their teeth" (23).

The long journey which constitutes the action of the book is reflected in the structure of the linear narrative which has no chapter breaks but a continuous sequence of paragraphs of varying length divided by line spaces and occasional ellipses. The intervals in which the characters set camp to rest or to protect themselves from natural or human peril are usually pointed by line separations indicating the passage of time, while the ellipses mark events of greater import involving their encounters with other people. The narrative structure in which "[t]he movement of the travelers and the movement of the text are one,"[10] also includes dream sequences and philosophical meditations on the part of the man. The expressive mode of the novel is that of a third-person limited omniscient narrative voice, and the inner voice of its protagonist is represented through frequent interior monologues. The fragmented words and phrases in the parts where stream of consciousness narration is employed in order to provide access to the man's mind, make interpretative attempts challenging as sentences reflecting the man's mind lack coherence, and float aimlessly in a temporal zone in which the meaning of the present is lost where the past and the future have become indistinguishable: "Query: How does the never to be differ from what never was?" (32). As the world seems to have come close to its end, and the idea of progress has been reduced to a journey the outcome of which is not even predictable, so are the words suspended in darkness, leading nowhere. The linguistic universe which seems to have lost its referents is at the brink of disintegration, and the narrative is replete with instances of the protagonist's struggle with speech:

> He tried to think of something to say but he could not. He'd had this feeling before, beyond the numbness and the dull despair. The world shrinking down about a raw core of parsible entities. The names of things slowly following those things into oblivion. Colors. The names of birds. Things to eat. Finally the names of things one believed to be true. More fragile than he would have thought. How much was gone already? The sacred

idiom shorn of its referents and so of its reality. Drawing down like something trying to preserve heat. In time to wink out forever. (93)

The narrative has also its moments of Hemingwayesque description of activities carried out by the man when he fixes things, uses tools or improvises utensils:

> He found a beer bottle and an old rag of a curtain and he tore an edge from the cloth and stuffed it down the neck of the bottle with a coathanger. This is our new lamp, he said. [. . .] he took the screwdriver and punched a hole in one of the cans of oil and then punched a smaller one to help it drain. He pulled the wick out of the bottle and poured the bottle about half full. [. . .] He twisted the cap off the gascan and he made a small paper spill [. . .] and poured gas into the bottle [. . .] took the rag and stuffed it back into the bottle with the screwdriver. He took a piece of flint from his pocket and got the pair of pliers and struck the flint against the serrated jaw. (143-4)

In passages like this the language becomes mimetically transparent and the "care with which the actions are described matches the care taken over the actions themselves, a characteristic matching of style and meaning."[11] In the lengthy and detailed description of the activities the sentences are precise and grammatically complete as opposed to the syntactic pattern of fragmentation in the descriptions of nature and natural phenomena as well as in the passages that convey the man's thoughts, feelings, memories, and dreams. In addition there are many instances of the man's impressions of his surroundings where the narrative voice seems occasionally to merge with the character's voice, making it even more difficult for the reader to locate the point of view:

> He lay listening to the water drip in the woods. Bedrock, this. The cold and the silence. The ashes of the late world carried on the bleak and temporal wind to and fro in the void. Carried forth and scattered and carried forth again. Everything uncoupled

from its shoring. Unsupported in the ashen air. Sustained by a breath, trembling and brief. If only my heart were stone. (10)

As in *Falling Man*, the third person narrator's description of the setting in *The Road* is often presented from the perspective of character. However, DeLillo's narrator engages the reader in the challenging task of re-configuring the scene of disaster from the fragmentary impressions and flashbacks of memory of his traumatized character whereas McCarthy's writing implicates a narrator armed with a concealed discursive authority, resulting in a narrative voice that seems to know more than what it discloses, and leaves its protagonist and reader alike in half-dark in the ruins of a devastated world. Although the events in the plot as well as some descriptive remarks about the landscape are related by the same narrative voice, it is chiefly from the man's limited perspective that we are allowed to see and make sense of them to the effect that voice and perspective become, at times, difficult to distinguish:

> When it was light enough to use the binoculars he glassed the valley below. Everything paling away into the murk. The soft ash blowing in loose swirls over the blacktop. He studied what he could see. The segments of road down there among the dead trees. Looking for anything of color. Any movement. Any trace of standing smoke. He lowered the glasses [. . .] and then glassed the country again. Then he just sat there holding the binoculars and watching the ashen daylight congeal over the land. (2-3)

The unnamed man of *The Road* takes pains to see "anything of color. [a]ny movement. [a]ny trace of standing smoke," (3) and his limited eyesight is due to the diminished light compared to "the onset of some cold glaucoma dimming away the world" (1). Thus, the motif of impaired vision implied by the "cold glaucoma" pertains not only to the man's inability to see his surroundings clearly, but also to his incompetence to make sense of the disaster that has befallen him. Notwithstanding the limitations of its political horizon, *Falling Man* provides the ground for discussions concerning the disastrous event of 9/11 by giving voice to conflicting world views whereas the one interpretive code the protagonist of *The Road* seems to possess is an ideological discourse inherited from a foregone time, and consequently fails him in his attempt to comprehend the horrifying new reality in which he finds himself. The man's inability to see is emphasized by the frequent use of the binoculars which repeatedly recur throughout the text, and the narrative techniques employed reinforce the sense of blurred vision suffered by the displaced protagonist. The man's surveillance of the landscape often concludes with a remark confirming the loss of vision: "Nothing to see" (7). Tim Edwards reads *The Road* intertextually with Ralph Waldo Emerson's *Nature*, which "in a sense provides a framework for discussing McCarthy's novel."[12] Both texts present landscape as text; Emerson's transcendentalist manifesto "sees the natural world as an edifying text, even a sacred text, a source of poetry and metaphor and truth,"[13] privileging the sense of sight thanks to which man communicates with Nature. The images of the "transparent eyeball" and "the sun" in Emerson's text appear in McCarthy's text "which is also threaded through with a network of ocular references as well as significant references to the sun."[14] However, the eye's function is pointedly diminished in the novel, and the sun "variously described as "alien," "lost," and "banished" is notable chiefly for its absence."[15]

Accompanying the image of impaired sight thus woven into the fabric of the text in which the man tries to hold on to the spatial coordinates provided by a diminished sun, is a weakened perception of temporality, further contributing to the man's incompetence in grounding himself in reality. In the morning when the narrative time starts with, the man looks "towards the east for any light" (1), and "with the first gray light", he scrutinizes "the country to the south": "Barren, silent, godless. He thought the month was October but he wasnt sure. He hadnt kept a calendar for years" (2). The man does not know for sure which month of the year they are in, or even which year it is, and the narrator withholds the information that could fill in the blanks left by the man's point of view. Keith in *Falling Man*, too, lives incognizant of the passage of time—although his entrapment in an eternal present is a choice he has made. However, DeLillo's narrator takes care to insert frequent temporal references indicating the days, weeks, months and years that have passed after the event, thus keeping the reader grounded in the historicity of the action.

DeLillo's *Falling Man* opens into "a world, a time and space of falling ash and near night" (3); *The Road*'s is a world of "nights dark beyond darkness and the days more gray each one than what had gone before," (1) with "the ashes of the late world carried on the bleak and temporal winds to and fro in the void" (10). The setting in *The Road* extends the image of the Ground Zero in *Falling Man* to "a wholly imagined realm of global annihilation."[16] Nevertheless, McCarthy locates his imagined setting in the South, a choice which is accounted for by the man's hope that the climactic conditions will be more accommodating there and that even some kind of life may have continued to exist. *The Road*, as Chris Walsh reads it, "is a novel deeply concerned with the geocentric myths and narrative patterns that have long been the domain of much American literature, especially literature of the South."[17] Thus McCarthy rewrites the mythic South which "as physical space, imaginative entity and narrative focus acts as a redemptive agency when all else seems to have vanished," but his descriptions of the cauterized landscape the father and son travel through implicate a South which is no longer "some pastoral sanctuary," but "a bleak, lifeless and threatening post-apocalpytic horror-scape which is entirely in keeping with the ideologically dystopian moment of the novel's composition and publication."[18]

Cant contends that "*The Road* seems to reflect the mood of fear that has permeated the Western mind in the first decade of the twenty-first century."[19] Indeed, fear is the driving force of the action in the novel in which as Jay Ellis notes "the word "scared" appears seventeen times in the boy's dialogue."[20] The fear haunting McCarthy's characters counterbalanced with the mournful mood and the poetic language in which their story is told is symptomatic of an ideological discourse on which a particular definition of civilization is based. Hence the prevalence of the elegiac mood in *The Road* in which the loss of the civilized world is heartbreakingly lamented, and in which civilization assumes the position of a transcendental signifier in the discursive frame to which the man subscribes. In the absence of an historical perspective civilization remains an unproblematic concept for the main character and not even once in the text does he question the inevitable connections between civilization and the catastrophe that has forever destroyed it. Reminiscent of the mood of Nina Bartos in *Falling Man*, who laments that "in these past days we've lost a thousand years," (44) the man's nostalgia for the world he once inhabited leaves room for nothing but grief over the loss of referents for civilization: "The frailty of everything revealed at last. [. . .] The last instance of a thing takes the class with it" (28). The chief character's ideological short-sightedness implied by his inability to see clearly is accentuated by the narrator's silence concerning the source and nature of the catastrophe of which the only account is provided in one single paragraph:

> The clocks stopped at 1:17. A long shear of light and then a series of low concussions. He got up and went to the window. What is it? she said. He didnt answer. He went into the bathroom and threw the lightswitch but the power was already gone. A dull rose glow in the window-glass. He dropped to one knee and raised the lever to stop the tub and then turned on both taps as far as they would go. She was standing in the doorway in her nightwear, clutching the jamb, cradling her belly in one hand. What is it? she said. What is happening?
>
> I don't know. (54)

Critics have labeled the catastrophe variously as a nuclear bomb, or a meteoroid hitting the earth, and both guesses stand within the range of plausibility. Cant has his doubts about the indication of a nuclear disaster, as none of the people in the novel displays symptoms of radiation sickness, and holds that "the nuclear holocaust is itself a metaphorical explanation for the state of the world that McCarthy creates as his wider metaphor for the condition of man in the realization of his cosmic insignificance."[21] At one point in the novel the man remembers the early days following the catastrophe: "People sitting on the sidewalk in the dawn half immolate and smoking in their clothes. Like failed sectarian suicides. Others would come to help them" (32-3). But "within a year," there were "fires on the ridges and deranged chanting," "the screams of the murdered," "the dead impaled on spikes along the road" (33). So even if the disaster was originally a divine retribution, it was apparently exacerbated by human violence. Thinking of the brutally murdered victims, the man speculates: "What had they done? He thought that in the history of the world it might even be that there was more punishment than crime but he took small comfort from it" (33). In his criticism of McCarthy's novel Kenneth Lincoln comments on the text's participation in the reinforcement of dominant ideology fueling the rhetoric of war that reduces historical questions to the fight between good and evil:

> No one wants to talk realistically about the end of the world, and for that reason we may just hasten the fire next time— fomenting war with lies and political machinations and imperial overreach; masking nuclear holocaust in the Rapture or Islamic terrorism (destroy a culture to save it); hiding Global Warming behind Creationism or job loss rationalizations; dismissing pandemics as mythical plagues in faraway places; blaming gays and liberals and scientists and soft politicians for antipatriotic bad news and sentimental social programs and godless biological research [. . .] Ronald Reagan said we could survive nuclear winter if there were *shovels enough to go around,* and the Second Bush administration wants to restart a Star Wars first-strike shield for Homeland Security that a trillion dollars won't make right. "Blessed *is* he that readeth, and they that hear the words of this prophecy, and keep those things which are written therein: for the time *is* at hand" (Revelation 1: 3).[22]

Given the text's resistance against historical clarity and contextual explanation, the time of the disaster which "is precisely stated with an emblematic intensity,"[23] is noteworthy in that it points at The Bible as one of its intertexts: the numbers in the hour "1:17" evoke Revelation 1:17 and the dream vision of John the Divine in which he witnesses the Second Coming of Christ. Critics have noted the allusion to Revelation as well as the boy's embodiment of messianic qualities implying the moral purity of Christ.[24] Steven Frye comments on the parallels between the novel's description of the catastrophic moment and John's recollection of his dream in verses 16-17:

> Christ's face is compared to the sharp "light" of the sun, implicitly "shearing" in its association with the "two-edged sword," holding stars that will appear throughout the novel as the man and the boy continually look past the gray and wasted world into the night sky. It is an image of power and destruction as well as hope and light, and it speaks both comfort and commandment, with Christ demanding that his presence be recorded in words, the allusion suggesting that the novel as parable is a kind of prophesy. In verse 19, Christ continues: "Write the things which thou hast seen, and the things which shall be hereafter."[25]

In addition to the religious discourse in which the ardent hearted man appears to find justification for his "mission" to carry the "light" embodied in his "son"—"Golden chalice, good to house a god" (78)—the biblical allusions and references, reinforced by the waste land imagery, calls for a reading of the novel as a parable. The imagery employed in the description of characters—"old world thespian" (8); "mendicant friars sent forth to find their keep" (133); "storybook peddler from an antique time" (185); "pilgrims" (193)—is redolent of the characteristics of the traditional lament narratives in which a righteous person is subjected to a tragedy whereby he loses all he has and turns to God, praying humbly to be restored to prosperity. The stylistic and thematic affinities *The Road* has, in particular, with The Book of Job in the Old Testament have been discussed before pointing The Book of Job as another major intertext of McCarthy's novel.[26] At the narrative level both texts engage with human suffering; the nameless man of the novel is as much universal a figure as Job to allow for a reading in which the particular characteristics of the hero seem to be less important than the group or type that he stands for. Similarly both texts can be said to participate in a certain form of journey narrative in which the hero is subjected to a disaster the reasons of which are unbeknownst to him, and is forced out of his familiar habitat into a desolate territory, creating the context for a spiritual journey. Both men have been "betrayed" by their wives in the course of their journey; the biblical Job is advised by his wife to "curse God, and die"[27] as she sees no point in repentance because her husband has not sinned, and as for the wife in the McCarthy novel, she has argued against her husband's decision to carry on, suggested death as the only solution for all three of them, and finally has killed herself. The words "curse God and die," come from the man as he contemplates the option his wife had suggested: "Can you do it? When the time comes? When the time comes there will be no time. Now is the time. Curse God and die" (120). The main difference between the two fictional men is that Job has been singly punished whereas McCarthy's man is one among the victims of a global catastrophe. Besides, Job is alone on his journey, having lost all his children, whereas the man is accompanied by his son and seems to care more for the boy's well-being than his own. The Book of Job contains Job's dialogues with his three elderly friends, and a young stranger named Elihu, who offer their views and counsel Job on his plight; the man in *The Road* usually converses with his son and the only other person to counsel him is an old man who calls himself Ely. Job finally hears the voice of God through the whirlwind, before he is restored to prosperity and dies in peace; the man in *The Road* dies in expectation of a divine intervention, and hoping, but not knowing for sure, that his son will be safe from perils.

These and other parallels with The Book of Job are too obvious to miss; more interesting, however, is the fact that in both texts the suffering individual's acute pain goes unrecognized—except, perhaps, by the feminine figures who see death as the only way to put an end to it—making accountable their arrogant anger directed at God. Thus Job, steeped in dust and ashes, addresses God: "Is it good unto thee that thou shouldest oppress, that thou shouldest despise the work of thine hands, and shine upon the counsel of the wicked? Hast thou eyes of flesh? Or seest thou as man seeth?"[28] Similarly the man in *The Road*, kneeling in the ashes with his face turned to the sky, sounds like a modern day Job, who, because his belief in divine justice has been shaken, seeks an explanation from God for the tragedy that has unjustly befallen him: "Are you there? He whispered. Will I see you at the last? Have you a neck by which to throttle you? Have you a heart? Damn you eternally have you a soul?

75

Oh God, he whispered. Oh God" (10). The acute pain experienced both spiritually and physically—both men are severely afflicted by a disease—is exacerbated by banishment. Job becomes an outcast from the God-blessed social community he has once belonged to, and has to live in a desolate landscape depicted in terms borrowed from desert imagery. Likewise, the man in *The Road* wanders with his son in a post-catastrophic desert-like world, a "barren, silent, godless" (2) land which is the diametrical opposite of a former conception of the world created by a generous and benevolent God.

These and other parallels suffice to evidence the dialogic relationship that *The Road* participates in with The Book of Job. However, the narrative forms in each text must be taken into account to evaluate the treatment of the Biblical tale in the novel. Bakthin has taught us that literary genres are distinguished not only by stylistic differences but more importantly by different thought forms and discourses rooted in historical contexts.[29] Given the huge differences between the historical cultural paradigms in which the two texts have been produced, differences of genre demand consideration concerning the interaction between Job's parable and McCarthy's "post-apocalpytic parable," dramatizing "the viability of faith in the face of an apparently Godless world."[30] It is true that the sufferers in both texts nevertheless sustain their belief in God although they fail to understand God's intentions. One major difference requires attention however; unlike the framing prose tale that begins and ends the narrative in The Book of Job, there is no framing narrative in *The Road* that would assure the reader that God does indeed exist and it is also solely in his might to mete out disaster and punishment as well as reward. The distraught sufferer in the Biblical text cannot understand why God has brought about his ruin, but the reader has already been informed through the framing prose narrative about the series of exchanges between God and Satan that will lead to Job's devastation. However unconvincing or unjust the reasoning behind it may seem to the modern reader, the framing tale leaves no doubt that it is God who authorizes Satan to ruin Job's life in order to test his faith and see whether he will end up cursing God, as Satan claims, when he is deprived of his wealth and health. By contrast, the third person narrator in *The Road* is reticent about the cause of the catastrophe, even refrains from providing an accurate account of the way it has happened, and is reluctant to share the man's faith in God and in the boy's messianic assignment: "He knew only that the child was his warrant. He said: If he is not the word of God God never spoke" (3). It is the character, and not the narrator, who knows and says. Besides, that the man knows that his son is his warrant is a recuperation of an earlier assertion made by his wife: "But he knew that if he were a good father still it might well be as she had said. That the boy was all that stood between him and death" (29). The man's insistence on his son's messianic assignment can be seen, therefore, as his way of justifying his will to survive, as has been expressed again by his wife:

> The one thing I can tell you is that you wont survive for yourself. I know because I would never have come this far. A person who had no one would be well advised to cobble together some passable ghost. Breathe it into being and coax it along with words of love. Offer it each phantom crumb and shield it from harm with your body. As for me my only hope is for eternal nothingness and I hope it with all my heart. (59)

The wife who appears only in the man's memories and his conversations with his son chooses suicide because she sees that "there is no stand to take" that could motivate her to carry on, and her husband has "no argument because there is none" (59). The wife's straightforward suggestion of a "passable ghost" as an excuse to live is to be more ironically echoed in what seems to be an obscurely philosophical argument by Ely, the old man they come across halfway in the text, who contests the man's claims concerning his son:

> When I saw that boy I thought I had died.

> You thought he was an angel?

> I didn't know what he was. I never thought to see a child again. I didn't know that would happen.

What if I said that he's a god?

The old man shook his head. I'm past all that now. Have been for years. Where men cant live gods fare no better. You'll see. It's better to be alone. So I hope that's not true what you said because to be on the road with the last god would be a terrible thing so I hope it's not true. Things will be better when everybody's gone. (183)

The character who calls himself Ely in *The Road*—he later says he has just made the name up—is interestingly comparable to the Elihu figure in The Book of Job: The biblical Elihu is a young man, and his youth is emphasized to mark him as an angelic mediator between God and man; he can communicate to both in his double-bound duty to persuade the sinner to pray, and ask God to show mercy to the penitent. As opposed to the discourse of Job's three elderly friends who fail to counterbalance Job's arguments concerning the injustice of God, Elihu adopts a more innovative strategy to thwart Job's complaint by transposing the issue onto an entirely different discursive frame: the relationship between God and man cannot be modeled on one between man and man, therefore it is not a matter of give and take, and piety and righteousness do not necessarily warrant exemption from misfortune. Thus canceling out Job's demand for a just trial, Elihu, instead, entices Job to appreciate God's might as manifested in his creation as a whole, leading him to eventually divest himself of his pride rooted in self-centeredness. In Carol Newsom's insightful reading of The Book of Job as a polyphonic text, Elihu is perceived as a dissatisfied reader, who arrives belatedly in the text and finds himself in the middle of a discussion which he finds too narrowly framed and to which he feels compelled to contribute with a new perspective unknown to the other participants.[31] Elihu is, Newsom maintains, at once a character in the narrative and a reader from a relatively more recent horizon of expectations—hence his belatedness marked by his young age—than the one hitherto occupied by both Job and his friends. Elihu's function in The Book of Job is one of defamiliarization intended to question Job's self-righteous assumptions concerning his place in the universe, which is rooted in a particular historical discourse, but passes as transhistorical, thus natural:

> What Elihu touches on here, without being fully aware of it, is the issue of the exhaustion and renewal of human discourse. How is it that human culture never finishes with what it has to say about perennial issues of existence? There are, to be sure, moments of pause, when it seems that everything that can be said has been said, but those moments do not last.[. . .] A stalled conversation is reinvigorated by someone eccentric to the original discourse. In recent years we have become increasingly aware of the invigorating potential of the eccentric speech of persons differentiated by gender, ethnicity, social class, and so forth. But even if participants were indistinguishable on those grounds, the sheer historicity of human existence would suffice to renew speech.[32]

Like the biblical Elihu, the Ely figure in *The Road*, who looks like "some storybook peddler from an antique time," (185) does not feel at home within the parameters of a discursive universe that seems to fall short of providing answers to existential questions—"I'm past all that now. Have been for years" (183). Unlike Elihu, however, Ely in the novel is an old man whose age testifies to a vaster experience of the world—"God knows what those eyes saw" (180). His speech about God is conspicuously ambiguous, and he dismisses the man's belief in God in a somewhat cryptic language, apparently speaking from a different paradigm than the man's: "There is no God. [. . .] There is no God and we are his prophets" (180-81).[33] Therefore, Ely can be said to have a similar, and certainly more conspicuous, metafictional function when looked at from the same perspective that Newsom sees the Biblical Elihu. In his role as the man's audience Ely is not only dissatisfied by what he hears but also refuses to be part of the text the man desperately tries to (re)produce. That is why, he explains, he has made up the name Ely, and will not disclose his real name: "I couldnt trust you with it. To do something with it. I dont want anybody talking about me. To say where I was or what I said when I was there. I mean, you could talk about me maybe. But nobody could say that it was me. I could be anybody" (182).

Thus the man's perspective from which the narrative seems to speak is challenged by first the wife and then Ely, who, like their counterparts in The Book of Job, threaten to disrupt narrative unity, which in the case of *The Road* seems to be more vulnerable due to the reluctance of its narrator to put things in perspective. In the absence of a narrative voice to confidently establish for the reader a more advantageous position in relation to the text's chief character whose relation to reality is highly problematic, the exchange of words between characters assumes an important part in the polyphony of the overall narrative. The lengthy mimetic interruptions at the diegetic level of the text are arguably the sites of contradiction where the narrative's claim to unity is challenged. The dialogues in the novel participate in a dialogic relationship with the man who remains trapped in the moral and religious discursive frame justifying his version of truth and rightful action, and "move[s] through the burning world like a distrustful Old Testament Yahweh, ready to kill other tribes that threaten him, not really very optimistic about the long-term goals, unable to love the other."[34]

The father-son dialogues in *The Road* can be said to allude to Platonic dialogues the purpose of which is to attain truth by means of an argument framed in answer and question form.[35] The dialogues in the novel are usually framed in a similar way and are aimed at the affirmation or confirmation by the boy of what his father takes to be the truth. The father's words are intended to establish a perspective from which the boy is meant to understand and acknowledge the mental and moral parameters in which his father's motives, convictions and actions are grounded. They are the good guys carrying the fire of civilization set against the evil forces represented by the bad guys:

We're going to be okay, arent we Papa?

Yes. We are.

And nothing bad is going to happen to us.

That's right.

Because we're carrying the fire.

Yes. Because we're carrying the fire. (87)

However, the exchanges also reveal the dynamics of the relationship between the two moving from a mentor-apprentice alignment to discordance which grows increasingly manifest in the boy's questioning of the justifiability of his father's convictions and moral attitude toward others. The encounters with other human beings present ramifications regarding the father's position. In the first of these interactions, they come across a man struck by lightning who is "as burntlooking as the country," with one eye "burnt shut," and his hair "a nitty wig of ash upon his blackened skull" (51). The boy wants them to help the man but the father responds, "No. We cant help him. There's nothing to be done for him" (51). The boy is upset with his father's indifference to the dying man's pain and would rather be dead. (56) The second encounter involves a "roadrat" from a group of scavengers, who is alone in the weeds relieving himself. The man and the roadrat engage in some negotiating discourse, each trying to measure the threat the other poses. The roadrat grabs the boy and holds his knife against his throat and is subsequently shot dead by the father, "with blood bubbling from the hole in his forehead" (68). The boy is horrified and refuses to talk to his father. As Jay Ellis remarks:

> McCarthy's latest apocalypse shows us one of the early acts of Revelation, where the forces of darkness seem to be winning [. . .] But the limitations of violence against even such a palpable evil are exposed: the father loses his humanity in his fear of inhumanity. It is the son [. . .] who risks being devoured because he cannot give up his feeling for strangers.[36]

Not long after the "roadrat" episode, the boy comes across a boy, "about his age, wrapped in an out-sized wool coat," who runs away from him in fear (88). The boy asks his father to go after him, because he is "afraid for that little boy," and is ready to "give that little boy half of [his] food" (90). The father responds, "Stop it. We cant" (90). The memory of the little boy, his double, his mirror image—"a face was looking at him" (88)—stays until the end with the child who is "scared that he was lost" (300). The next encounter involves a horrifying sighting of people held captive in the basement of a plantation house waiting to be slaughtered and eaten. The scene with the man stepping down into the basement with a lighter in his hand, "[swinging] the flame out over the darkness like an offering" reads like a dark parody of Plato's fable of the cave with slaves chained together in darkness:

> Huddled against the back wall were naked people, male and female, all trying to hide, shielding their faces with their hands. [. . .] Then one by one they turned and blinked in the pitiful light. Help us, they whispered. Please help us. Christ, he said. Oh Christ. (116)

The man turns and grabs the boy, rushing out in horror and they narrowly escape the approaching group of cannibal inhabitants of the house. The man who claims to be carrying the fire tellingly "drop[s] the lighter," in his haste and later tells his son that he meant to go back to "try and lead them away," but he did not because he could not leave the boy alone. The dwellers of the basement are not lead by the "light" to "truth" as the dwellers of Plato's cave are, probably because McCarthy's man lodges at his heart a disbelief growing stronger than his faith. In one of the houses the man picks up a book from the cluster of "soggy volumes in a bookcase," but the darkness of the "livingroom partly burned and open to the sky" makes it impossible for him to read as there is "no way to light" the candle he has found in a drawer (138). Strikingly it is after he puts the book back in frustration that he has a moment of epiphany which manifests itself in terms of absence of light and as the diametrical opposite of Plato's promised insight into truth:

> He walked out in the gray light and stood and he saw for a brief moment the absolute truth of the world. The cold relentless

circling of the intestate earth. Darkness implacable. The blind dogs of the sun in their running. The crushing black vacuum of the universe. (138)

The episode with old Ely reveals further the man's indifference to other human beings sharing the same plight as opposed to the boy's self-sacrificial attitude towards them. Notwithstanding the previously discussed affinities the old man has with the biblical Elihu, his name also invokes another biblical figure, that of Elijah, "the promised passover guest for whom there is always a door open and a place set at the table," and who "fed by ravens and a widow in a time of famine (1 Kings 17), functions as an archetypal *hôte* who both receives and dispenses hospitality in a Levinasian reflection of God."[37] McCarthy's man sees that the old man "sitting like a starved and threadbare buddha," (179) poses no threat whatsoever but he remains reluctant to help him until the boy insists, "Maybe we could give him something to eat" (173). It is again the boy who understands that the half-blind old man is "scared" (173). As Jay Ellis has noted, the boy uses the word "scared" three times for other people including the little boy, the old man, and even the thief they encounter along the road.[38]

The man's treatment of the thief who steals their belongings they have temporarily left unattended is probably the cruelest of his acts. When he catches up with the thief he makes him, on threat of death, take off all his clothes and then leaves him in the road "standing there raw and naked, filthy, starving" (275). The thief has done nothing the man would not do as he puts it: "I'm starving, man. You'd have done the same" (275). His son's protests compel the father to go back to the spot to return the thief's clothes, but they cannot find him. When the man tries to assure his son that he "wasnt going to kill him," the boy replies: "But we did kill him" (278). The discordance between them reaches a climax when the father tries to calm down his son, saying, "You're not the one who has to worry about everything," to which the boy replies, "Yes I am [. . .] I am the one" (277).

Their next encounter with other people, which comes soon after the episode with the thief, presents a familial relationship mirroring certain aspects of the relationship between the father and son. In an abandoned town they are passing through the father is wounded by a man shooting arrows from the upper window of a house, and subsequently shoots the bowman with a flare gun, severely wounding him. When the father goes into the house he finds a woman holding the wounded man in her arms, who begins to curse the father for what he has done. She has "taken off her coat to cover him," and when the father intimates that the other people in the house have remorselessly left her alone, she declares her caring commitment to the wounded man: "I left myself here" (283). The bowman's violence targeted at a human being he probably takes to be the "enemy" and the woman's protectiveness for the person she cares for reflect on both the father's cruelty and his protective behavior towards his son.

The man's perspective which is left unquestioned by the narrative voice is exposed to be debatable through the boy's questioning of his father's treatment of the others. His faith in his father's righteousness begins to waver as the man's acts begin to contradict what he preaches, and the boy asks in frustration, "Are we still the good guys?" (81). Similarly, his ultimate refusal to hear his father's stories is grounded in his understanding that "in the stories we're always helping people and we don't help people" (287). The man's "old stories of courage and justice," (42) involving good guys against bad guys which he keeps telling his son—although we never get to hear any of those stories—have their sources in a broader range of identificatory narratives encompassing the categories of good and evil. Functioning as ideological state apparatuses, these narratives help establish national, religious, ethnic identities at the political level, and re(produce) the dominant ideology in which they are born.

As a fictional engagement with the questions concerning American (Western) identity in the political climate of post-9/11, *The Road* reinstates the hegemonic assumptions of global capitalism. However, it is also replete with symptoms of an anxiety revealing the unsaid that emerges in the gaps and blanks that disrupt the text's claim to unity, and exposing the ways in which the constructed notions of identity and civilization are embedded in the political discourse of global hegemony. That the father in *The Road* has been interpellated in an Althusserian sense to identify with the good guys of ideology is obvious; more importantly however, in his role as "Father" he acts as the embodiment of dominant ideology, the voice that interpellates. His stories are meant to more than comfort and encourage his son; they supplement his account of their mission. The father tries to hold the boy in the discursive space of ideology he himself takes refuge in against all odds symbolized by the tarpaulin he uses as a shield against cold and rain. As the plastic material of tarpaulin is what makes it efficient as a "cover" in their struggle against Nature, the force of ideology rests in its "plasticity", in the fact that it is a discursive construct that masks reality and thrusts the individuals into an imaginary relation to their reality. Hence, after having killed a man, the man reasserts his justified position: "You wanted to know what the bad guys looked like. Now you know. It may happen again. My job is to take care of you. I was appointed to do that by God. I will kill anyone who touches you" (80).

Whoever the bad guys in the father's stories are, the bad guys in the novel are frequently referred to as the cannibals and are the absolute others from whom the father and son must stay away in order to survive. Jay Ellis writes:

> They encounter the backward hungry heathen tribes that would eat them, that would succumb to the latest feeling that the end is nigh by rejecting the forward progress from mere predatory cannibalism, to the literal sacrifice for magic reassurance that God is on our side—and therefore against another tribe—and on to the symbolic sacrifice and its collapse of binaries. The world of *The Road* really is one of two kinds of people. The father and son in the novel stay on the road less out of some hope of a better place, than out of a spiritual (which is to say optimistic beyond the bounds of reason) hope for a better space; they might find people who do not eat people. People who carry the fire of civilization.[39]

Thus the good and the bad guys who are equally subjected to a permanent state of hunger due to dreadful natural conditions are divided by a line between those who eat men and who do not, and the good guys may be forced to kill the bad guys in order not to be eaten by them. So when the father shoots to death a man who threatens his son's life with a knife his act is made justifiable on the grounds of the latter's insinuated cannibalism. After having killed the man who is referred to as the "roadrat" by the narrator, the father takes his son away in fear that others from the diesel truck might come after them, but returns later to the site to retrieve their belongings and sees what is apparently the remains of the dead man, cooked and eaten by his fellow travelers: "Coming back he found the bones and the skin piled together with rocks over them. A pool of guts. He pushed at the bones with the toe of his shoe. They looked to have been boiled. No pieces of clothing" (74).

In her study of the significance of cannibalism in another McCarthy novel, *Blood Meridian*, Judie Newman discusses the fictional manifestations of the primordial fear of being hunted by predators that determines the ways in which characters relate to cannibalism.[40] According to the theses put forward by ethologists, Newman maintains, the hunted man precedes the hunting man, and at the foundation of civilization is this fear of being eaten by predators, the discovery of fire giving the man the upper hand in the struggle against Nature, and turning him from the status of prey to that of the hunter. The episode, in which the father murders the man in *The Road* considered in the light of that argument, is arguably the closest the man comes to face that primordial fear of being eaten and, thanks to the "fire" he possesses, ends up a murderer. Importantly, the oscillation between narration and dialogue throughout the episode puts the reader in an uneasy situation as regards the motives of both parties. The episode begins with the narrator's account of how the diesel truck men are viewed by the man:

> [W]hen he looked back toward the road the first of them were already coming into view. God, he whispered. [. . .] They came shuffling through the ash casting their hooded heads from side to side. Some of them wearing canister masks. One in a biohazard suit. Stained and filthy. Slouching along with clubs in their hands, lengths of pipes. Coughing. Then he heard on the road behind them what sounded like a diesel truck. [. . .]

When he raised to look up he could just see the top of the truck moving along the road. Men standing in the stakebed, some of them holding rifles. (62-4)

After the truck rattles and stops on a slope the man sees that "coming through the weeds twenty feet away was one of their number unbuckling his belt" (64). Although, as it turns out, the "lean, wiry, rachitic" (65) roadrat's intention is nothing but to defecate, the protagonist regards him as a potential threat, a predator looking "like an animal inside a skull looking out the eyeholes," (65) and holds his pistol on him. Taken by surprise, the diesel truck man then manages to grab the boy and threatens to cut his throat, after which the man shoots him to death. The narration of the action in the scene is accompanied by a series of exchanges following the movement of the shifting power relations between the two men, blurring the distinction between the categories of the hunter man and the man hunted. Although the diesel truck man has already been identified as one of the hunting men with firearms, initially it is the protagonist with a gun in his hand who is in the position of the hunter in relation to the roadrat who has been caught in a vulnerable situation. His sense of superiority is revealed in the intimidating manner he interrogates the man: "What do you mean you don't know? Take the mask off"; "You don't know where you're going?"; "I told you not to look back there" "That's a lie"; "That's what you think" (66). In addition, the protagonist who literally carries the fire—the gun—as opposed to the diesel truck man who is without fire, is shown to be adorned with another kind of fire, the light of scientific knowledge. The "roadrat" tries to deter the man saying his fellow travelers will hear the sound if he shoots him:

You aint got but two shells. Maybe just one. And they'll hear the shot.

Yes they will. But you wont.

How do you figure that?

Because the bullet travels faster than sound. It will be in your brain before you can hear it. To hear it you will need a *frontal lobe* and things with names like *colliculus* and *temporal gyrus* and you wont have them anymore. They'll just be soup.

Are you a doctor?

I'm not anything. (66-7) [Italics mine.]

It is that power/knowledge axis that sustains the apparently medical-savvy man's superiority over his rival whose ignorance and inferiority is implicated in his speech, and whose inadequate reasoning in calculating the power balance brings about his death. Consequently, driven by the fear of being hunted, the protagonist becomes the hunting man, aided by fire literally and justifying his deed with his mission: "This is my child, he said. I wash a dead man's brains out of his hair. That is my job" (77). The blurring of the distinctions between the two men, hunted and hunter, is implied as the man later refers to his victim as "my brother":

This was the first human being other than the boy that he'd spoken to in more than a year. My brother at last. The reptilian calculations in those cold and shifting eyes. The gray and rotting teeth. Claggy with human flesh. Who has made of the world a lie every word. (79)

The image of fire and its concomitant light conventionally associated with civilization and progress from the Promethean myth to the grand narrative of Enlightenment is thus linked with its inevitably destructive aspect, implicated in the act of murder committed by the man who is literally armed with fire and who believes he and his son are carrying "the fire". Lincoln writes: "Prometheus stole fire from the gods for human use, differentiating the raw from the cooked, and for that impudence he was chained to a rock where each day a vulture ate out his liver. Civilization followed, eventually God's holocaustal *fire next time*."[41] Indeed, the novel is replete with references to the conflictual nature of fire; throughout the journey the father and son pass through burnt down cities and landscapes covered in ash and dust while their survival depends largely on the maintenance of fire against cold and dark. An apocalyptic fire has destroyed their world, yet they hold on to the idea of a redemptive fire carried within and meant for not only their survival but for the good of humanity. However, in spite of his conviction in the spiritual fire, which signifies "civilization being passed from father to son,"[42] and which gives meaning to his struggle for survival the man seems not to care in the least for other people who share the same post-apocalyptic predicament; in fact his lack of compassion leads to acts of cruelty towards others.

Given the historicity of McCarthy's novel in terms of its production and reception in a post 9/11 world in which the "War on Terror" rhetoric is used to mask a reckless capitalist aggression, the understated presence of oil in the text constitutes the most significant symptom of the ideology that maintains its reality effect by making a distinction between good and evil, and threatens to reveal the disturbing realities concerning the lost civilization. On the first day of their journey in the narrative the man and the boy come upon a roadside gas station; the gas tank for the pumps is emptied out, yet the pumps with their hoses are "oddly still in place" (5). It is at this specter of a gas station where the man tries to "smell the pipe but the odor of gas [is] only a rumor, faint and stale," that he picks up a dead phone and dials the number of "his father's house in that long ago," (5) in a gesture linking oil to his memory of a familial idyll. To borrow from Wesley G. Morgan's essay "The Route and Roots of *The Road*", the route the father has chosen "would hardly be the most direct way to the southern coast."[43] Given that the man has "an oil company map that he frequently consults," his choice of route is hardly accidental and it seems that "he is planning the trip through Knoxville, and nearby places, as a way of acquainting his son with his roots."[44] Later in the novel the man remembers how he "pored over maps as a child, keeping one finger on the town where he lived": "Just as he would look up his family in the phone directory. Themselves among others, everything in its place. Justified in the world" (194).

What the man can salvage from the remnant of the gas station is nothing more than a half quart of motor oil he drains from plastic oilbottles "for their little slutlamp to light the long gray dusks, the long gray dawns (6)". On the second day of the journey they pass through a city "mostly burned," with "no sign of life," where a dried corpse in a doorway is "grimacing at the day," a reminder of a bygone civilization like the "cars in the street caked with ash [. . .] fossil tracks in the dried sludge (11)". Later, while looking at the roads on the map the boy says, "But there wont be any cars or trucks on them," which the father confirms with a definitive "No" (44). There may be no motor vehicles left running on the titular road of the novel, and cars, trains and caravans may appear as the ghosts of a civilization running on petrol, yet oil is there, like a potent signifier which seeps throughout the text at various instances, albeit in mostly dissipated forms like the gasoline, the motor oil the protagonists use for their lamp, the gas in the lighter or the plastic tarpaulin—oilcloth is a derivative of oil after all—which they use as a shelter from cold and storm.

In discussing the oil allusions in *The Road*, the significance of the map that guides them during the journey should not be overlooked either; it is a map of the states—or what is left of them. Morgan's meticulously studied essay traces the route followed by father and son, identifying the specific locations they pass through along the journey, including Middlesboro, Kentucky, Knoxville, Tennesy, Cherokee and Franklin, North Carolina, and Pendleton, South Carolina.[45] More importantly, however, the map of the states on which the man relies for the accomplishment of his mission is an oil company map. Those two markers—the U.S.A. and the oil company—charge the map with an extra-textual political import which permeates the text and disrupts the father's self-justified discourse. It should not be surprising then the first edifice the protagonists come across in the narrative is the remains of a gas station. In its dystopian vision reflective of the post-9/11 mood, McCarthy's writing unwittingly places oil at the origin of the tragedy despite its protagonist's adherence to the rhetoric of "Us against Them", good guys against bad guys, civilization against barbarism. It is perverse indeed "that the scorched earth which *The Road* depicts often brings to mind those real apocalypses of Southern Iraq beneath black oil smoke, [. . .] not unconnected with the contemporary American regime."⁴⁶ Tellingly, whereas the one motor vehicle that appears functional in the narrative belongs to the "bad guys"—the ruthless barbarous cannibals who possess the truck and the oil, the real thing—the "good guys" are left only with tarps, motor oil cans, and the oil company map that accompany them like the specters of a bygone civilization. With its Biblical overtones and yearnings for a lost civilization, McCarthy's narrative, grieves over, yet cannot do so without producing breaches that subject to question that civilization.

To go back to the map, like the political entity it denotes, the "tattered oilcompany roadmap" has fallen apart in time and its unity can be maintained by the numbers the man has written with a crayon on the corners of its separated leaves "for their assembly" (43). As Walsh maintains:

> Phone books, maps, states and even nations have no signifying purpose in the fictional world presented to us here, and road signs advertising the tourist attraction of Rock City stand isolated where all signifiers of previous order, place and supposed security lack any kind of signifying purpose.⁴⁷

The journey to the south is taken under the guidance of that disintegrating map, a text itself from an earlier discourse—that of the nation state; although its signifiers may still refer to faintly recognizable signifieds, the change in context has irrevocably modified its meaning:

> These are our roads, the black lines on the map. The state roads.
>
> Why are they the state roads?
>
> Because they used to belong to the states. What used to be called the states.
>
> But there's not any more states?

No.

What happened to them?

I dont know exactly. That's a good question.

But the roads are still there.

Yes. For a while. (43-4)

Considering that the symbolism of the map points out the fact that nation as a politically constructed entity has fallen apart as the states (commonly used as an abbreviation for the U.S.A.) no longer exist, the stamp of the oil company the map bears expands the symbolism to reflect on the links between the pre-apocalyptic concept of nation and its auxiliary ideology of patriotism, and the hegemonic economy-politics of the U.S.A. bound by the interests of global capitalism led by the world's greatest oil companies. The father still holds on to the signs on the map disconnected from their original context in the same way as he insists on the value of his stories, which like the map, belong with an outdated discourse, the narrative that DeLillo has already proclaimed to have ended "in the rubble."[48] It is the boy, not surprisingly, who comes to realize the hollowness of that narrative, and protests against his father's stories because "[t]hose stories are not true," and they are not "like real life" (286-7).

The man's rhetoric of "Us against Them" is most poignantly subverted in the episode where he mistakes his own image in the mirror for the "enemy":

> At the farther edge of the town they came upon a solitary house in a field and they crossed and entered and walked through the rooms. They came upon themselves in a mirror and he almost raised the pistol. It's us, Papa, the boy whispered. It's us. (139)

The boy's "It's us, Papa" reaches far beyond their images in the mirror to reflect on their commonality with nearly all the other human beings they come across in the course of the journey. Suggestive of the Lacanian mirror constitutive of the subject's perception of self and other, the mirror here serves as the medium through which the dependence of identity on difference is established. The man's sense of self derives from the hierarchical logic of the self-same according to which the other is constructed as the inferior opposite, and partakes of the discourse that is at the heart of his self-righteousness. The mirror motif underlining the man's (mis)recognition of himself appears earlier in the novel with the chrome motorcycle mirror attached to the shopping cart, and at which the man keeps looking to see the images of the others who might be out there to kill them. Thus, as the man mourns for the loss of the civilized world the distinction between self and other is projected as an antagonism between the civilized and the barbarian. The persistent emphasis on the impairment of vision discussed earlier thus exposes it to be an introjected blindness of the man. It is the boy who often sees things before his father does even though the latter is usually aided by the binoculars, and it is the boy again, not surprisingly, who insists on the need for an alternative way of relating to the others.

The mirror episode arguably constitutes a site of resistance in the text against the reinstatement of the hegemonic discourse on which globalization's claims and political maneuvers depend, and which presents the West "as the privileged vanguard of an evolutionary process that applies to all nations."[49] Although both the good and the bad guys in *The Road* are Americans, the distinctions between them are made on the basis of civilized versus barbarian opposition. When the man mistakes his image for the barbarian other, the "enemy" is domesticated, not unlike the Bill Lawton/Bin Laden doubling in *Falling Man*, and casts doubt on the self-same identity of the civilized. McCarthy's man on the road takes pains to maintain the rituals of civilization in the face of most inhuman conditions, although his fight for survival involves acts of scavenging, stealing, and even killing. In their first morning in the novel his breakfast preparations simulate table manners; he spreads the tarpaulin on the ground "for a table," on which he lays "plates and some cornmeal cakes in a plastic bag and a plastic bottle of syrup" (3). This is a highly significant gesture, "for despite their condition as scavengers in a seemingly cataclysmic world, he performs the centuries-old ritual of preparing the meal as a sign of civilized humanity," in a world "where barbarity and the threat of cannibalism continuously loom."[50] Another item the man places on the "table", however, is the loaded pistol, which is, as Randall S. Wilhelm observes, "an iconic image that encapsulates the mindset of the violent culture of dominance from which ostensibly the world-threatening catastrophe has originated."[51] Following on the mirror imagery, the image of the pistol is a disruptive agent that holds a mirror revealing the inherent violence underlying civilization.

In *Falling Man* DeLillo's characters anxiously and obsessively talk about the possible causes of the event that constitutes the core of his narrative. McCarthy's novel prophesizes about the end of the world without offering any discussion of the nature of the catastrophe that has brought the world to an end. In spite of this narrative choice which places the focus on the consequences rather than the causes of the imagined global disaster, however, there exist in the text disturbing symptoms of a certain version of civilization synonymous with the consumer culture of late capitalism. In a sense the whole novel can be read as a dark parody of consumerism, a shopping venture in dire circumstances with the shopping cart emerging as the reminder of a way of life driven by an irresistible urge for consumption. It is as if the entire landscape of the novel has turned into a derelict supermarket in the labyrinthine aisles of which they desperately move with the sole aim of grabbing things and loading their shopping cart. If the lost society was a consumer's paradise, the desolate universe of the novel is nothing but a consumer's nightmare in which one has got hold of a shopping cart but can no longer enjoy the full bliss of carelessly overloading it. Of course, the sight of the man and the boy in rags clutching the handlebar of the dislocated trolley points to the underside of that paradise as Jay Ellis has noted: "Whom do you see on the streets out there, pushing a shopping cart? The homeless."[52]

The can of Coca-Cola they come across in the ashen land stands as an ironic memorial to that lost paradise of which the boy knows nothing and for which the father mourns. The father hands over the can of Coke to his son in anticipation of an appreciative response, and to his relief, the boy takes a sip and says "it's really good" (23). As Alan Warner remarks, "[an] uncomfortable, tellingly national moment comes when the father salvages perhaps the last can of Coke in the world. This is truly an American apocalypse."[53] The episode involving one of the rare jubilant scenes in the novel is disturbingly reminiscent of myriads of television commercials broadcast daily all over the globe that one can hardly avoid reading into it the extra-textual connotations of the brand name as a symbol of the global force of capitalism. Representative of not only a particularly American way of life but of a particular form of civilization glorifying consumerism, the iconic image of the can of Coke emerges, in the dystopian world of *The Road*, as a symptom pointing at the ills of a greedy global capitalism ready to do whatever it takes in its endless pursuit of more of the world's markets.

The illusory nature of ideology that interpellates individuals as consuming subjects reveals itself most succinctly in the episode beginning with their discovery of the house in which the man initially mistakes his image in the mirror for the (hostile) other. In the yard of the house they enter in the hope of finding food, they come upon an underground bunker which contains "the richness of a vanished world" (147). The bunker "walled with concrete block," (146) has been built in anticipation of disaster, "because someone thought it might be needed" (147). It is filled with "crate upon crate of canned goods. Tomatoes, peaches, beans, apricots. Canned hams. Corned beef. Hundreds of gallons of water in ten gallon plastic jerry jugs. Paper towels, toilet paper, paper plates. Plastic trashbags stuffed with blankets" (146). "I found everything", the father cries out to his son, "everything. Wait till you see" (147). The protagonists are briefly allowed to have a glimpse of an oasis-like experience whereby they find themselves in "this tiny paradise," (159) a mock haven of plenitude with overstuffed shelves, which seems to have been built on the model of that inglorious supermarket.

The timing of the bunker episode in McCarthy's slow-moving plot in which the same daily routine of survival is repeated with little variation is crucial. The feeling of relief in the episode is experienced at exactly that point in the narrative when the reader's empathy for the father is at its highest as he keeps vigorously trying to keep his son alive and safe at the end of a week of hunger and exhaustion—"How many days to death?" Ten? Not so many more than that. He couldnt think" (141). Thus, the explicit mood of surprise and delight in the exchange between the father and the son is arguably aimed at manipulating the reader to unquestioningly enjoy the plenitude and safety the bunker provides:

> What is all this stuff, Papa?
>
> It's food. Can you read it?
>
> Pears. That says pears.
>
> Yes. Yes it does. Oh yes it does. (147)

As they go "along the rows of stenciled cartons," of "chile, corn, stew, soup, spaghetti sauce," replicating "the richness of a vanished world," the boy asks in astonishment: "Why is this here? [. . .] Is it real?", to which the man responds, "Oh yes. It's real" (147). However, as the initial amazement at the shelves of processed food and household supplies, and other domestic facilities including a chemical toilet gives way to an ironic semblance of pre-catastrophic daily routine—eating, sleeping, bathing decently—the bunker is revealed as the microcosm of a way of life deemed blissful and fulfilling, yet maintained in a constant state of fear and anxiety. The bunker's metonymic relation to the house to which it is linked spatially, is transposed into the domain of the metaphor as it is a purpose-built and modest replica of the original. Those metonymic and metaphoric correlations between the two edifices betray the assumptions of an underlying ideology experienced by the individual subjects as reality. Understood in Althuserrian terms, then, ideology is made visible in the fictional universe of *The Road* in which the bunker appears as a symptom of that ideology, magnifying disproportionately the inherent fear of an hostile Other, which may be variously specified as a political, global, climactic, nuclear, chemical, or heavenly threat with catastrophic potency, ready to destroy "civilization", a term divested of its historicity and political contingency by that very invisible ideology that promotes, by naturalizing, the world-views, moral values and the form of social relations required and imposed by an increasingly globalised hegemonic capitalism. The underground edifice in which the man and his son take temporary refuge from the hostile others, specified here as the cannibalistic tribes, the hordes of thieves, and scavengers, serves its purpose as a refuge in the face of threat, while at once functioning as a symptom of the ideological unconscious of the house of which it is the underside.

The dinner the father and son have in the bunker adds more to the novel's response to the disturbing questions concerning the fragility of the ideological universe constitutive of American identity. As the protagonists imitate in the bunker the cordial domestic routines of daily life associated with civilization as it was once presumably experienced in the house, the boy thanks to the inhabitants of the house, probably long dead by now, emphasizing their connection in the manner of a thanksgiving prayer: "Dear people, thank you for all this food and stuff. We know that you saved it for yourself and if you were here we wouldnt eat it no matter how hungry we were and we're sorry that you didnt get to eat it and we hope that you're safe in heaven with God" (155). Although the thanksgiving prayer proper is addressed to God for providing food for the family/community, the boy's addressee is the absent people who once inhabited the place. Despite his unawareness of a long history of violence and injustice constitutive of his civilization, the boy's phrasing invokes the historical origins of the ritual in his thanks to "the people who gave us all this" (154).

The house belongs with the Lacanian Symbolic, the order of lived social reality that can only be sustained by avoiding the disturbing presence of its underneath, the Real that threatens to expose its constitutive inconsistencies and antagonisms. The protagonists' entry into the house is initiated with their recognition of themselves in the mirror, which is translatable in Lacanian terms to the Mirror Stage where a sense of subjectivity begins to form through identification with the image on the surface of the mirror. The subject is thus split from the beginning for the image is already an Other, and the recognition of the self always a misrecognition. Hence the father's mistaking his image for a threatening Other in the Symbolic, which is the house. The underground bunker, the at once familiar and strange underneath of the house is the avoided Real, the site of destructive fantasies that structure and support the social reality lived in the house. Recalling Freud's notions of the "uncanny" (*unheimlich*), and the "return of the repressed," the bunker functions, by its very presence, as a reminder of the fragility of the house and its dependence on what it tries to escape from. In his controversial essay on 9/11, Slavoj Zizek wrote:

> The fact that the September 11 attacks were the stuff of popular fantasies long before they actually took place provides yet another case of the twisted logic of dreams: it is easy to account for the fact that poor people around the world dream about being Americans—so what do the well-to-do Americans, immobilized in their well—being dream about? About a global catastrophe that would shatter their lives—why? This is what psychoanalysis is about: to explain why, in the midst of our well-being, we are haunted by nightmarish visions of catastrophes.[54]

Once the "nightmarish visions of catastrophe" haunting the owners of the house who had built the bunker in anticipation of an external threat come true, and the bunker is actually used by the survivors of a real catastrophe that has taken place "at home", the bunker emerges as the site where the fantasy which "structures the excess that resists our immersion in daily reality"[55] is traversed, and the discomforting contradictions of the ideological universe embodied in the image of the bunker are revealed.

After having spent a couple of days in the bunker, which provides a semblance of the lost civilized world, the man is woken one night by a dream in which he is visited "by creatures of a kind he'd never seen before" (163). Once the plenitude of the man's civilization is approximated in the house's underground, the destructive fantasy constitutive of that civilization's unconscious makes a return and the pre-catastrophic fears and anxieties reappear in the guise of strange creatures who, the man thinks, "perhaps had come to warn him": "Even now some part of him wished they'd never found this refuge. Some part of him always wished it to be over" (163).

The Road is a full-scale immersion in fantasy in an effort to traverse the "nightmarish visions of catastrophes" much greater in scope than the events on 9/11. In order to spot the anxiety accompanying the fantasy of destruction it might be helpful to look at the background story concerning the novel's genesis:

> The Road had its genesis in a very specific moment, when McCarthy had checked into an old hotel in El Paso with his young son, John [. . .] and stood looking at the still city at two or three in the morning from the window of their room, hearing the lonesome sound of trains and imagining what El Paso "might look like in fifty or a hundred years." "I just had this image of these fires up on the hill and everything being laid waste and I thought a lot about my little boy. And so I wrote those pages and that was the end of it." [. . .] This image of a wasted El Paso seems to have been fixed in his memory in conjunction with that of his small boy sleeping in the bed behind him—an image of paternal care, the father standing guard between his son and the world outside, between his son and a future that implied the loss of the world of the father's memory. [. . .] In the writing process, the emotional grounding of the novel, the city of the father's past, which he and his son travel through and away from, mutated from El Paso to Knoxville, the town of McCarthy's own boyhood.[56]

McCarthy's remarks made in a television interview and included in the above quotation have been viewed by other critics too as evidencing a biographical link between the writer and his son. Although the interpretation of a literary work cannot be reduced to the writer's autobiographical explanations the author's words are illuminating of the ways in which future projections of "everything being laid waste" are grounded in the anxieties of the current historical moment. The unnamed protagonist of the novel seems indeed to be representative of the "well-to-do Americans" whose fantasies of global destruction McCarthy's novel manifests.

The microcosmic image of the house in *The Road*'s nightmare vision appears in forms that attest to the loss of home as a confined place in which one feels safe from danger. The houses which the man and the boy come across throughout the novel are half-burnt down, their roofs are missing, interiors plundered, and whatever has remained is covered in ashes and dust, reeking of cadavers and body waste. Early in the novel when the father takes his son to the "old frame house with chimneys and gables and a stone wall," which is where he has grown up," the boy is afraid to go in because "[t]here could be somebody here" (24-5). The man leads his son into the ruined house and the empty rooms telling him about the Christmases of his childhood but the boy "watche[s] shapes claiming him he [cannot] see" (26). They come upon the "bones of a small animal dismembered and placed in a pile," in the livingroom, and when in what used to be his room the man pushes open "the closet door half expecting to find his childhood things," he sees a "[r]aw cold daylight [falling] through from the roof," "[g]ray as his heart" (27). Home is not a place to return to, and the homecoming narrative is given a final ironic twist at the conclusion of the passage: "I am sorry. [. . .] We shouldnt have come" (27).

Another house they come across is the plantation house, "tall and stately with white doric columns across the front," and a "port cochere at the side," where they discover the captives in the basement (111). The mansion with its "failed pretensions to order and stability from another era,"[57] has become home to the cannibalistic tribes of post-apocalypse. Jay Ellis observes that in McCarthy's novel "[t]he domestic space as a place of loving family is entirely obviated, and displaced by the meat-locker basement that recalls several post-Vietnam 70's horror films," in which "the American domestic is the site not of refuge from lawless terror, but the site of lawless terror."[58] True, but that place of loving family has always been maintained at the cost of other lives as the history of slavery is evoked in what appears to be a passing remark in the description of the house: "Chattel slaves had once trod those boards bearing food and drink on silver trays" (112). The house still serves as a refuge for its current inhabitants who have replaced the slave-owners of the past, and has already been a site of terror for the chattel slaves who have been replaced by the people kept as livestock in the basement.

Therefore just as the house with the underground bunker reveals the repressed fear and anxiety existing simultaneously with feelings of comfort and security, the plantation house exposes order and stability to be maintained by a constant supply of disposable human beings. The house as microcosm for country defined in terms of a territory occupied by a nation is torn down in this dystopian narrative only to bring out its underlying structure. With the collapse of the Symbolic order represented by the house image, the laws and rules of conduct to which the father desperately remains attached are no longer viable. Consequently, the concomitant form of nation and national identity is shown to have dissipated too, as the man's ruined family house suggests the undoing of the familial/national idyll to which no return is possible. This point is further underscored in the text when the man casts aside his billfold containing his "driver's license"—a government-issued identity paper—and his "money and credit cards"—the markers of an economic order sustaining that identity (52). As in *Falling Man*, the family as national metaphor in *The Road* is obliterated, as the man finally discards his wife's photograph in the billfold. However, in DeLillo's novel the mother and child remain together in their isolated world whereas the mother in the McCarthy novel is present through her absence, and haunts the father and son in their thoughts and dreams.

The wife/mother in the novel has killed herself to avoid the possibility of witnessing her child being tortured, raped or eaten by tribes of men who use "women for nothing more than to birth babies straight to the spit," yet "her abandonment of her own child [. . .] to the thanatotic world of men, a world of fire and literal sacrifice and cannibalism haunts the novel."[59] The absence of the maternal body in the text leaves the child in *The Road* in the domain of the father and subjected to his language and law he tries to recover from the ruins of the Symbolic. After having disposed of his wife's photograph along with his billfold containing money, credit cards, and his driver's license, the man contemplates: "He thought about the picture in the road and he thought that he should have tried to

101

keep her in their lives in some way but he didnt know how" (56). The boy, upset because his father has refused to help the man struck by lightning, expresses his discontent in the form of a wish to return to the mother:

> I wish I was with my mom.
>
> He didnt answer. He sat beside the small figure wrapped in the quilts and blankets. After a while he said: You mean you wish that you were dead.
>
> Yes.
>
> You musnt say that.
>
> But I do.
>
> Don't say it. It's a bad thing to say.
>
> I cant help it.
>
> I know. But you have to.
>
> How do I do it?
>
> I dont know. (56-7)

The boy's wish to go back to the mother, to the pre-symbolic maternal Real where language does not exist is an expression of the failure of the male Symbolic from which the woman has been banished like "the banished sun circl[ing] the earth like a grieving mother with a lamp" (32). At the end of the journey the maternal space returns in the symbolism of the sea, the longed for destination which, in a sense, emphasizes the journey's regressive trajectory. The seascape is like "the desolation of some alien sea breaking on the shores of a world unheard of," and the ocean is "vast and cold and shifting heavily like a slowly heaving vat of slag and then the gray squall line of ash" (230). The maternal space returns only in the form of a "bleak sea," which is "[c]old," "[d]esolate," and "[b]irdless," and holds no promise other than a sunken sailboat ironically named "Pajaro de Esperanza" (Bird of Hope) (239). In his first dream at the opening of the novel, the man wanders in a cave led by the child "[l)ike pilgrims in a fable swallowed up and lost among the inward parts of some granitic beast" (1). The womb metaphor suggested by the cave and elaborated by the image of water, "a black and ancient lake," hosting "a creature," with "its bowels, its beating heart," and its "brain that pulse[s] in a dull glass bell," inscribes the maternal body at the beginning of the narrative (1-2). The creature in the dream is both the mother and the child, and is without speech: "It swung its head from side to side and then gave out a low moan and turned and lurched away and loped soundlessly into the dark" (2). The moaning evokes the subconscious level of language associated with the maternal repressed by the symbolic order of the male which McCarthy's entropic narrative shows to have failed humanity. On the day before his death, the father admits to his failure by accepting that his son has been right all along: "You're the best guy. You always were" (298). Jay Ellis contends:

> The father has confessed his sins to the son, by telling this story, in which the father's actions begin to worry the son that perhaps the father is no longer, after all, one of "the good guys." The father's vigilance, his handiness with fear, has led him to play it safe to the point that life itself can be preserved and yet its meaningfulness dim away.[60]

The dream at the beginning of the narrative returns in the final pages, "encroach[ing] upon the waking world," with water "dripping [. . .] in the cave," and with "[t]racks of unknown creatures in the mortified loess": "In that cold corridor they had reached the point of no return which was measured from the first solely by the light they carried with them" (300-301). By the end of the narrative the reversal of roles implied in the dream in which the child leads the father comes true as the boy looks after his dying father. The narrative of the journey closes upon itself with the return of the man's first dream implying a regression to the maternal body in the avoided Real that cannot be articulated in language. It is where both the father's life and his narrative end.

Three days after his father's death the boy comes across a man, "dressed in a gray and yellow ski parka," and carrying "a shotgun upside down over his shoulder," with "a nylon bandolier filled with shells for the gun" (301). He is a man the father would possibly not find trustable: "A veteran of old skirmishes, bearded, scarred across his cheek and the bone stoven and the one eye wandering. When he spoke his mouth worked imperfectly, and when he smiled" (301). However, the shotgun man not only helps the boy burry his father but offers to adopt him into his family including another little boy and a girl (304). The scene rewrites the one in which the boy's own father had refused to take responsibility for the little boy whom his son had seen earlier in the novel, and who is, significantly the subject of their last exchange:

> Do you remember that little boy, Papa?
>
> Yes. I remember him.
>
> [. . .]
>
> But who will find him if he's lost? Who will find the little boy?
>
> Goodness will find the little boy. It always has. It will again. (300)

At the end of the novel goodness seems to have found the boy. However the conclusion of the text is highly ambiguous; the sudden arrival of the man and the family at the end of the novel appears as *dues ex machina*, a contrived closure forced upon the narrative which depicts the "ponderous counterspectacle of things ceasing to be," (293) in "[b]orrowed time and borrowed world and borrowed eyes with which to sorrow it (138). The concluding image is that of the child attended by a mother figure:

> The woman when she saw him put her arms around him and held him. Oh, she said, I am so glad to see you. She would talk to him sometimes about God. He tried to talk to God but the

best thing was to talk to his father and he did talk to him and he didnt forget. The woman said that was all right. She said that the breath of God was his breath yet though it pass from man to man through all of time. (306)

The narrative voice does not explain why the woman so warmly welcomes the boy; it is not that they are without child as the man who has found the boy says there are another boy and a girl in their company. Whether this God-believing woman has seen in the boy some divine quality as his father did is not clear. In the same way, the statement that God's breath passes from man to man belongs to the woman, and not to the narrator. The one thing the reader knows for sure is that the boy "tried" to talk to God, but preferred to converse with his dead father to remember him. The novel ends with a coda in which any promise of a new world is eclipsed by the elegiac vision:

> Once there were brook trout in the streams in the mountains. *You could see them* standing in the amber current where the white edges of their fins wimpled softly in the flow. They smelled of moss in your hand. Polished and muscular and torsional. On their backs were vermiculate patterns that were maps of the world in its becoming. Maps and mazes. Of a thing which could not be put back. Not be made right again. In the deep glens where they lived all things were older than man and they hummed of mystery. (307) [italics mine.]

It is not clear who is speaking here, and to whom. Is it the absent God, finally stooping to talk directly to (the) man, as God does in The Book of Job? Or, is it the narrator, who decides, in a sudden change of mind at the end of the narrative, to directly address, and implicate the man and/or the reader—the "you" of the paragraph—in the text at a point where the story has already ended? Is it the woman who "would talk to [the boy] sometimes about God" speaking about God and his mysterious ways manifested in his creation, exemplified here by the trout? Or finally, is it the father posthumously telling his son of a world which is no more, and of which the mystery is mapped on the backs of "brook trout in the streams in the mountains"? The "trout swaying in the current" links the concluding passage to one of the father's cherished memories. Earlier in the novel as they are walking in the mountains they reach a spot where the man remembers having once watched trout as a boy: "He stood on a stone bridge where the waters slurried into a pool and turned slowly in a gray foam. Where once he'd watched trout swaying in the current, tracking their perfect shadows on the stones beneath" (30). The elegiac mood of the final paragraph lamenting for "a thing which could not be put back," and "[n]ot be made right again," obscures the global catastrophe in a cloak of mystery incomprehensible to all but the trout: "in the deeps glens where they lived all things were older than man and they hummed of mystery" (307). The prelapsarian image of "trout in the streams" is in sharp contrast to the wasteland traversed in the narrative which now directs its gaze at life's beginning in water, before man and before language. However, trout do not exist anymore and never will, nor will the world encrypted in the patterns on their backs be put back and made right again.

The apocalyptic vision of an unrecoverable world in the closing coda "undercuts whatever hopeful ending the boy's rescue has promised."[61] The contrived happy ending of the journey narrative is reminiscent of the tragic form which conventionally concludes with the old order having been replaced by a new one: The father is dead, the boy has learned the means of survival from his father but will not repeat his mistakes, and has found a new family with an apparently different set of moral values and rules at the end of the journey. However, there is no guarantee that the boy and the family will survive the consequences of the catastrophe. The text does not end where the journey ends but returns to the dystopian vision it has maintained throughout. At its conclusion, the text strives for monologic closure with an ultimate recourse to the lament form suturing over its inconsistencies and contradictions. The disappearance of the human in the final elegiac paragraph forecloses the possibility of any meaningful human action which could reverse things and make a better place of the world. "After America", comes the "darkness implacable".

NOTES to PART II

1 Cormac McCArthy, *The Road* (Picador, London, 2007). All subsequent references will be made to that edition.

2 Tim Edwards, "The End of the Road: Pastoralism and the Post-Apocalyptic Waste Land of Cormac McCarthy's *The Road*," in *The Cormac McCarthy Journal* (Vol.6, Autumn 2008), 59.

3 John Cant, *Cormac McCarthy and the Myth of American Exceptionalism* (Routledge, New York and London, 2008), 266.

4 Cant, 331.

5 Alan Warner, "The Road to Hell," *The Guardian*, 4 November 2006. http://www.guardian.co.uk/books/2006/nov/04/featuresreviews.guardianreview4. Web. 13 January 2011.

6 Chris Walsh, "The Post-Southern Sense of Place in *The Road*," in *The Cormac McCarthy Journal* (Vol.6, Autumn 2008), 53.

7 Walsh, 48.

8 Cant, 332.

9 Warner.

10 Cant, 267.

11 Cant, 275.

12 Edwards, 56.

13 Edwards, 56.

14 Edwards, 57.

15 Edwards, 57.

16 Steven Frye, *Understanding Cormac McCarthy* (University of South Carolina Press, Columbia, 2009), 164.

17 Walsh, 53.

18 Walsh, 52.

19 Cant, 332.

20 Jay Ellis, "Another Sense of Ending: The Keynote Address to the Knoxville Conference," in *The Cormac McCarthy Journal* (Vol. 6, Autumn 2008), 29.

21 Cant, 269.

22 Kenneth Lincoln, *Cormac McCarthy: American Canticles* (Palgrave Macmillan, New York, 2009), 163.

23 Frye, 169.

24 See the discussions on the boy's messianic designation in William Kennedy's "Left Behind," in *NY Times Book Review* (8 October, 2006) and Philip Connors's "Crenellated Heat," in *London Review of Books* (25 January, 2007).

25 Frye, 169.

26 See for example, John Vanderheide, "Sighting Leviathan: Ritualism, Daemonism and the Book of Job in McCarthy's Latest Works," and Susan J. Tyburski, "'The Lingering Scent of Divinity' in *The Sunset Limited* and *The Road*," both in *The Cormac McCarthy Journal* (Vol. 6, Autumn 2008).

27 The Book of Job, ch.2, verse 9

28 The book of Job, ch.10, verses 3-4.

29 See Mikhail Bakthin and Paul Medvedev, *The Formal Method in Literary Scholarship: A Critical Introduction to Sociological Poetics* (Harvard U.P., Cambridge, 1985).

30 Tybursky, 121.

31 Carol A. Newsom, *The Book of Job: A Contest of Moral Imaginations* (Oxford U.P., Oxford and New York, 2009).

32 Newsom, 203-4.

33 Ely's declaration that "There is no God and we are his prophets," (143) is an inversion of the sentence from The Koran, "There is no God but Allah, and Muhammad is his Messenger." Referred to as "Kalimah" or "Shaadah" in Islamic discourse, it is the principal requirement of Islam, and is the last statement believers are supposed to make before death to be granted admission into Jannah (paradise). "Kalimah" means word and "Shaadah" means both witness and martyrdom in Arabic. Its inclusion in McCarthy's text is significant given the novel's thematic concern with death and its historical context. It also strengthens the argument that Ely's discursive paradigm is different from the man's, and may explain the lack of communication between them.

34 Ellis, "Another Sense of Ending," 30.

35 See Carole Juge's discussion in "The Road to the Sun They Cannot See: Plato's Allegory of the Cave, Oblivion, and Guidance in Cormac McCarthy's *The Road*," in *The Cormac McCarthy Journal* (Vol.7, No.1, 2009),16-30.

36 . Ellis, "Another Sense of Ending," 30.

37 Phillip A. Snyder, "Hospitality in Cormac McCarthy's *The Road*," in *The Cormac McCarthy Journal* (Vol.6, Autumn 2008), 81.

38 Ellis, "Another Sense of Ending," 30.

39 Ellis, "Another Sense of Ending,"30.

[40] Judie Newman, *Fictions of America: Narratives of Global Empire* (Routledge, London and New York, 2007), 132-49.

[41] Lincoln, 168.

[42] Cant, 270.

[43] Wesley G. Morgan, "The Route and Roots of *The Road*," in *The Cormac McCarthy Journal* (Vol.6, Autumn 2008), 46.

[44] Morgan, 46.

[45] Morgan, 39-47.

[46] Warner.

[47] Walsh, 52.

[48] DeLillo, "In the Ruins," 34.

[49] Manfred B. Steger, *Globalism: The New Market Ideology* (Rowman and Littlefield, Lanham, 2002), 13.

[50] Randal S. Wilhelm, "'Golden Chalice, Good to House a God': Still Life in The Road," in *The Cormac McCarthy Journal* (Vol. 6, Autumn 2008), 132.

[51] Wilhelm, 133.

[52] Ellis, "Another Sense of Ending," 32.

[53] Warner.

[54] Slavoj Zizek, "Passions of the Real, Passion of Semblance," in Zizek, *Welcome to the Desert of the Real: Five Essays on September 11 and Related Dates* (Verso, London and New York, October 2002), 17.

[55] Zizek, "Passions," 17.

[56] Dianne Luce, "Beyond the Border: Cormac McCarthy in the New Millennium," in *The Cormac McCarthy Journal* (Vol.6, Autumn 2008),9.

[57] Walsh, 53.

[58] Ellis, "Another Sense of Ending," 32.

[59] Ellis, "Another Sense of Ending," 29.

[60] Ellis, "Another Sense of Ending," 34.

[61] Edwards, 60.

BIBLIOGRAPHY

·························

Abel, Marco. *Violent Affect: Literature, Cinema, and Critique After Representation*. Lincoln: University of Nebraska Press, 2008.

Amend, Christoph and Georg Diez, "I Don't Know America Anymore," [This interview originally appeared in *Die Zeit* magazine on 11 October 2007. This English translation was done by dumpendebat of Dum Pendebat Filius.] http://dumpendebat.net/static-content/delillo-diezeit-Oct2007.html. Web. 24 April 2011.

Annesley, James. *Fictions of Globalisation*. London and New York: Continuum, 2006.

Aristotle. *Poetics* (translated with an Introduction by Gerald F. Else). Ann Arbor: The University of Michigan Press, 1994.

Arnold, Edwin T., and Dianne C. Luce, eds. *Perspectives on Cormac McCarthy*. Jackson: U.P. of Mississipi, 1999.

Bakhtin, Mikhail, and Pavel Medvedev. *The Formal Method in Literary Scholarship: A Critical Introduction to Sociological Poetics*. Translated by A. Wehrle. Cambridge: Harvard University Press, 1985.

Bartlett, Jen, "Cultivated Tragedy: Art, Aesthetics, and Terrorism in Don Delillo's *Falling Man*." 1-11. http://startrek.ccs.yorku.ca/~topia/docs/turningon/Bartlett.pdf. Web. 7 May 2011.

Baudrillard, Jean. *The Spirit of Terrorism*. Chris Turner (trs.). London: Verso Publications, 2003.

—. "Requiem for the Twin Towers," in Baudrillard, 35-48.

—. "The Spirit of Terrorism," in Baudrillard, 1-34.

—. "The Violence of the Global," in Baudrillard, 85-105.

Bloom, Harold, ed. *Cormac McCarthy*. New York: Infobase, 2009.

Borradori, Giovanna. *Philosophy in a Time of Terror: Dialogues with Jürgen Habermas and Jacques Derrida*. Chicago: The University of Chicago Press, 2003.

Boxall, Peter. *Don DeLillo: The Possibility of Fiction*. London and New York: Routledge, 2006.

Brauner, David, "'The Days After' and 'The Ordinary Run of Hours': Counternarratives and Double Vision in Don DeLillo's Falling Man," *Review of International American Studies* (Winter 2008/Spring 2009, 3.3-4.1), 72-81.

Cant, John. *Cormac McCarthy and the Myth of American Exceptionalism*. New York and London: Routledge, 2008.

Caruth, Cary. *Unclaimed Experience: Trauma, Narrative and History*. Baltimore: John Hopkins U.P. 1996.

Connors, Philip, "Crenellated Heat," in *London Review of Books* (25 January, 2007).

Cvek, Sven, "Killing Politics: The Art of Recovery in *Falling Man*," in *Studia Romanica Et Anglica Zagrabiensia* (Vol.54, Zagreb, 2009), 329-352.

DeLillo, Don. *Falling Man*. Basingstoke and Oxford: Picador, 2011.

—. "In the Ruins of the Future: Reflections on Terror and Loss in the Shadow of September," *Harpers Magazine*, December 2001. http://dumpendebat.net/static-content/delillo/DeLillo-Ruins_of_Future-Dec2001.pdf

Duvall, John N., "Witnessing Trauma: *Falling Man* and Performance Art," Chapter 10, in Olster, 152-168.

—, ed. *The Cambridge Companion to Don DeLillo*. New York: Cambridge U.P., 2008.

Eagleton, Terry. *Holy Terror*. Oxford, New York: Oxford U.P., 2005.

Edwards, Tim, "The End of the Road: Pastoralism and the Post-Apocalyptic Waste Land of Cormac McCarthy's *The Road*," *The Cormac McCarthy Journal* (Vol.6, Autumn 2008), 55-61.

Ellis, Jay, "Another Sense of Ending: The Keynote Address to the Knoxville Conference," in *The Cormac McCarthy Journal* (Vol. 6, Autumn 2008), 22-38.

—. *No Place For Home: Spatial Constraint and Character Flight in the Novels of Cormac McCarthy*. New York, London: Routledge, 2006.

Foer, Jonathan Safran. *Extremely Loud and Incredibly Close*. New York: Houghton Mifflin, 2005.

Frye, Steven. *Understanding Cormac McCarthy*. Columbia: University of South Carolina Press, 2009.

Hamid, Mohsin. *The Reluctant Fundamentalist*. Florida: Harcourt Books, 2007.

Herman, Judith. *Trauma and Recovery: The Aftermath of Violence: From Domestic Abuse to Political Terror.* New York: Basic, 1997.

Jameson, Fredric. *The Political Unconscious: Narrative as a Socially Symbolic Act.* London: Routledge, 2002.

Jenks, Chris. *Transgression.* London and New York: Routledge, 2003.

Juge, Carole, "The Road to the Sun They Cannot See: Plato's Allegory of the Cave, Oblivion, and Guidance in Cormac McCarthy's *The Road*," in *The Cormac McCarthy Journal* (Vol.7, No.1, 2009),16-30.

Junod, Tom, "The Falling Man," *Esquire* (September 2003). www.esquire.com.8September2009 Web. 5 January 2010.

Kauffman, Linda S., "Bodies in Rest and Motion in *Falling Man*," Chapter 9 in Olster, 135-151.

—. "The Wake of Terror: Don Delillo's "In The Ruins of The Future," "Baader-Meinhof," and *Falling Man*," *Modern Fiction Studies* (Vol.54, No. 2, Summer 2008), 353-377.

Kennedy, William, "Left Behind," in *New York Times Book Review* (8 October, 2006).

Lentricchia, Frank and Jody McAuliffe, "An Interview with Frank Lentricchia and Jodie McAuliffe," http://www.press.uchicago.edu/Misc/Chicago/472051in.html. Web. 9 July 2011.

Lentricchia, Frank and Jody McAuliffe. *Crimes of Art and Terror.* Chicago: The University of Chicago Press, 2003.

Lincoln, Kenneth. *Cormac McCarthy: American Canticles.* New York: Palgrave Macmillan, 2009.